PRAISE FOR *DATA DRIVEN*

Marketers today face huge disruption driven by new paths to purchase and an explosion of new technologies. This requires an entirely new playbook for harnessing the power of data and AI to create more relevant, engaging connections with consumers. *Data Driven* is a must-read guide for any marketing professional confronting this general challenge and seeking to drive top-line revenue for brands.

—DEANIE EISNER, President, Kellogg Company

In today's digital, data-driven world, marketers have the opportunity to actually *know* what their customers like, what they hate, and where they're headed—provided they are up to speed on the practical tools and helpful rules of thumb that Tom, Chris, and Vivek share in this book. *Data Driven* is an indispensable workbook for any marketing practitioner seeking to conquer these new possibilities.

—GEOFFREY MOORE, Venture Partner,
Mohr Davidow Ventures and Wildcat Venture Partners,
and bestselling author of *Crossing the Chasm*

If you work in a business that depends on digital interaction with consumers, much of what you thought you knew has been upended in the last 10 years. This book is one of the fastest ways to quickly learn what you need to know to succeed, with real-world examples and frameworks you can use to effectively engage your audiences.

—ALYSIA BORSIA, CMO and Chief Data Officer, Meredith Corporation

Data and AI are revolutionizing marketing, and Tom, Chris, and Vivek are among the pioneers driving this tectonic shift. This book is a terrific guide, full of unique insights for marketing and business professionals, and anyone else interested in how data is fundamentally transforming our world.

—Jonathan Levin, Philip H. Knight Professor and
Dean of Stanford Graduate School of Business

There has never been a more bewildering—or exciting—time to be a brand, and Chavez, O'Hara, and Vaidya are the smartest guides we've got. Whether you're a hard-headed marketer or just a curious soul, *Data Driven* shows you what makes modern data-driven brands succeed.

—Martin Kihn, VP Research, Gartner, Inc., and author of *House of Lies*

Data offers explosive competitive possibilities across every business sector, which is why investors are spending so much time wrapping their heads around it. *Data Driven* is an essential guidebook for anyone trying to separate hype from practical possibility, written by pioneers and experts who are ready to share what they know in terms the rest of us can quickly understand and apply. If you're an investor or an executive seeking to navigate new data-driven opportunities, this is a must-read.

—Nino Marakovic, CEO and Managing Director, Sapphire Ventures

If you're like many businesspeople, you're likely bumping into data-related topics at work but having a hard time parsing all the jargon. *Data Driven* is the fastest way to pierce through all the buzzwords and understand what data can practically do for your company and your career.

—Greg Schott, CEO, MuleSoft, A Salesforce Company

It's rare to have a chance to learn about a field from someone who combines the intellectual rigor of an academic, the ease of a good storyteller, the vision of an industry-changing entrepreneur, and the straightforward pragmatism of a company-building CEO. It is especially rare to learn about a subject as important, pervasive, and potentially confusing as data, particularly today. Tom, Chris, and Vivek bring all their considerable experience to deliver on that promise.

—Alex Rosen, Managing Director, Ridge Ventures

There are very few resources out there that can truly help newcomers and seasoned marketers alike make sense of the data-marketing landscape and hone their skills. This book does just that, and was very much needed. Praise to the authors who managed to demystify fairly complex topics in such a compelling and engaging way—this is no small feat!

—Vincent Balusseau, MBA, PhD, Associate Professor of Marketing, Audencia Business School

DATA
DRIVEN

HARNESSING DATA AND AI TO
REINVENT CUSTOMER ENGAGEMENT

TOM CHAVEZ
CHRIS O'HARA
VIVEK VAIDYA

NEW YORK   CHICAGO   SAN FRANCISCO
ATHENS   LONDON   MADRID
MEXICO CITY   MILAN   NEW DELHI
SINGAPORE   SYDNEY   TORONTO

1 2 3 4 5 6 7 8 9   LCR   23 22 21 20 19 18

ISBN   978-1-260-44153-6
MHID   1-260-44153-9

e-ISBN   978-1-260-44154-3
e-MHID   1-260-44154-7

Design by Lee Fukui and Mauna Eichner

McGraw-Hill Education books are available at special quantity discounts to use as premiums and sales promotions or for use in corporate training programs. To contact a representative, please visit the Contact Us pages at www.mhprofessional.com.

*To all the Krazies@Krux who believed and built
something great together—don't relent!*
—TC and VV

*To Noni Reed O'Hara, 79, who always believed in me,
and Mia Meredith O'Hara, 11, who inspires me
with her courage every single day.*
—COH

CONTENTS

PREFACE

ORIGINS

vii

INTRODUCTION

THE MAGIC COFFEE MAKER

xv

CHAPTER 1

THE EMERGENCE OF PEOPLE DATA

1

CHAPTER 2

THREE CORE PRINCIPLES FOR BUILDING
A WINNING DATA STRATEGY

33

CHAPTER 3

DATA IN, DATA OUT

55

CHAPTER 4

THE FIVE SOURCES OF DATA-DRIVEN POWER

85

CHAPTER 5

MAKING IT REAL FOR YOUR ORGANIZATION

127

CHAPTER 6

**THE NEW BASIS OF COMPETITION:
KNOW, PERSONALIZE, AND ENGAGE**

155

CHAPTER 7

**SEVEN FORECASTS TO LIGHT UP
YOUR FUTURE SENSORS**

169

ACKNOWLEDGMENTS

205

NOTES

211

INDEX

215

PREFACE: ORIGINS

People interested in business marvel at the meteoric rise of companies such as Amazon, Netflix, Google, and Facebook. Who knew that e-commerce, video streaming, search, and social networking could become so huge so fast? Pundits explain that it's an inevitable by-product of the growth of the Internet and our need to remain tethered to it. The more we connect, the more opportunities for the advertising, viewing, and selling that generate massive revenues for those companies.

Ubiquitous connectivity only partially explains the rise of the Internet giants and the surprising success of digital upstarts such as Spotify, Tinder, and Twitch. A powerful steel thread runs through all these companies. What they have in common is *data*: the ability to capture it—increasingly every scrap—and put it to work to generate insights, recommendations, and offers that dazzle their customers.

If you're in the business of engaging with existing customers or attracting new ones, you can run, but you can't hide from data. It is the fuel that enables any company to know its customers intimately, improve its products, deliver better customer service, optimize any business process, and predict the future direction of markets.

This book is about data—some of it difficult to see and capture, much of it hiding in plain sight. From our vantage point there's no reason why the possibility and power of data should remain a dark art practiced only by the high priests of the Internet. It's time to yank the covers back and demystify all of it.

We're not business school professors or pundits. We're practitioners with decades spent diving into data. More recently, we built a company called Krux, a data management system (also known as DMP, for "data management platform") that is now part of Salesforce. Today, companies like Adidas, Turner, L'Oréal, and Bloomberg depend on the Salesforce DMP to power their marketing, commerce, and advertising operations.

When we reflect on our journey over the last 20 years, it seems a little trite to reason backward from its outcome and say, "But of course." Data is considered the new oil, commentators remind us, and companies that extract, clean, analyze, and transport it are essential to the growth of every industry.

But many of the core concepts we discovered on the path to this data awakening weren't so easily taken for granted, especially when we were fire-testing them in the open market in 2010. Some of them were a little askew. Some of them are still unproven. But they powered us through the rough times, and on balance they mostly came to fruition. Alan Kay, the pioneering computer scientist, once said, "Context gets you 80 IQ points." Before hurtling forward, we'll follow Kay's dictum and offer some context for the observations and ideas in this book.

During the last two decades, partly because we're data geeks by training and disposition but mostly because we were lucky, we found ourselves at the center of the consumer data revolution. Early on we latched onto three core hypotheses, which dramatically shaped Krux's trajectory: first, it was possible to generate a 10x value increase through audience segmentation; second, a 1,000x cost-performance gain was within reach as compute power increased and the cost of data storage decreased; and third, the decoupling of user data from content, ads, and other digital interactions could enable a 360-degree, real-time view of every customer.

The prequel to Salesforce DMP and Krux was a company called Rapt, which was founded in 1999 and sold to Microsoft in late 2007. I was a founder and CEO, and Vivek was the CTO. By 2004 Rapt was helping large media publishers such as MSN and Yahoo! optimize the pricing of their advertising inventory, the rectangular slots on web pages that thousands of companies were purchasing to reach their desired audiences. Rapt's analytic engines determined optimal price points for Yahoo!'s advertising products, generally differentiated by the size and placement of the ad, the channel on which it ran (finance versus auto versus entertainment), and the time of delivery.

We noticed that a small cluster of Yahoo! salespeople in the finance vertical weren't adopting the prices that our analytic engines were generating. For the exact same ad inventory that their colleagues were selling at a $6 CPM (cost per thousand impressions, or *cost per mille*, where the "mille" is Latin for "thousand"), this group was commanding price points almost 10 times higher, and *their prices were attracting buyers*. It was unnerving. Much of our project's success depended on price discipline within the sales organization and shared confidence that our algorithms were homing in on the right price points. The group's activity wasn't a deployment issue to be ironed out but an insurrection to be put down.

We pushed for a deeper look and asked the rebels how they were able to sell a finance ad with a price recommendation of $6 to financial advertisers like Fidelity and Vanguard for $55. After some digging, they finally confessed that they weren't presenting it as an ad at all. Instead, they were selling it to their clients as an opportunity to engage with a particular audience segment: financial executives who make over $250,000, live on the Eastern Seaboard in Connecticut, and oversee portfolios worth more than $25 million.

There was very little chance that Yahoo!'s ad delivery technology at the time could reliably target ads with that level of precision. As hard-charging salespeople frequently do, the group was taking liberties. But it was the germ of something larger and ripe with possibility.

Segmentation is a concept that every marketing business school professor proclaims and every MBA learns, but here we were seeing clinical evidence of its effects outside the academy. Don't sell a rectangle on a screen; sell an opportunity to connect with a wealthy portfolio manager. Hypothesis #1—the idea that through segmentation, value differences of 10x were within reach—took root. Our task then was to industrialize what the group of Yahoo! sales renegades had done and to move it from the realm of freewheeling salesmanship into the gears of a day-to-day operation.

At the time, we were helping MSN, Microsoft's news and information site, with a similar deployment of our technology. We thought it would be powerful if we could store every interaction—every click, every page visit, every mouseover—for every MSN user, so we could feed the anonymized information to our pricing algorithms, which were hungry for data. Microsoft was the richest, most powerful company in the world. We wondered if the executives there would agree to foot the bill to store this data. We crunched the numbers and estimated the cost at about $850,000 per day, or around $310 million per year.

Microsoft was rich, but this was too rich. We set the idea aside and pressed on. But it was our second moment of truth and the beginning of Hypothesis #2: Was it possible to break the cost-scale barrier we were hitting at Microsoft?

The third hypothesis became clear during a critical meeting at Microsoft. A large, established marketing agency had negotiated an arrangement to buy very large quantities of advertising inventory on Hotmail from Microsoft at an attractive price. The agency had previously negotiated to pay a certain CPM, around $2.50, for targeting tied to age and gender. Without warning, one day the agency came to us and declared it was no longer interested in paying $2.50. It would take the ads "flat" and untargeted. It proposed $0.50 CPM as a suitable price for what it insisted was a substantially less valuable asset.

It was hard for us to disagree with its claim that untargeted e-mail was much less valuable, but the more vexing question for us was: Why was the agency doing that? *How* was it doing that? Didn't it need us to ensure that the ads were targeted to the people the agency was seeking to reach? After all, they were our users, and of course we kept our registration data under lock and key.

We didn't know for sure, but we started formulating a theory, soon to be validated, about what was afoot. Data about who the users were behind the screen was captured via little pieces of code called "cookies." The data answered questions such as: Had they started to buy something and abandoned a shopping cart? Did they click? Were they *even here*? For about a decade starting in 1996, the advertising that fueled the explosive growth of the Internet was tightly bound to the data stored inside cookies. There was nothing in the fundamental architecture of the Internet that required this to be so. It's just the way the cookie crumbled. (Sorry, couldn't resist.)

Principals within the advertising ecosystem started to realize in 2005 that the architecture of the Internet didn't require any binding of the ad to the user cookie. Data—in this case, the information stored in the cookie—could be fully decoupled from ads or any other content on the screen. It could be captured, analyzed, and mined for value entirely on its own. What became clear is that the agency negotiating with Microsoft had used the cookies to quietly build its own data pools for targeting users. It didn't need us to tell it who was on the other side of the screen; all it had to do was read its own cookies, which had been set by the computer code that we allowed the agency to slip into the ads running on Hotmail, another part of the story we'll get to later.

This led to Hypothesis #3: new market energy could be released if data were unshackled and allowed to flow freely across *every* customer experience, not just ads, and across every device, not just desktops, but mobile handhelds, tablets, toasters, refrigerators, cars, and other gizmos yet to be invented.

Fast-forward to today. Salesforce DMP, on behalf of our many clients, captures data that is over 100x the size that MSN was seeing in 2015 and that now costs 10x less. This represents an astounding 1,000x cost-performance breakthrough, achieved in just a decade. Companies as diverse as Georgia-Pacific, Adidas, Turner, and Kellogg's use DMP segmentation capabilities to create more relevant experiences with their customers. They have built centers of excellence dedicated to data and hired new analysts to mine data for insights, recommendations, and smarter strategies for consumer engagement. They're reengineering their customer-facing operations to take fuller advantage of predictive analytics and AI—all of it fueled by data.

When Warner Bros. launches a new action movie, no longer does the company pretend that it's the first action movie it has ever brought to theaters. Instead it looks into a huge reservoir of historical data about consumers who've engaged with action-oriented content from Time Warner across every screen and channel. The company harnesses the data to find existing fans, attract new ones, and usher all of them into the theater.

In the 1940s when Robert Oppenheimer led the Manhattan Project in the high desert of New Mexico, he grasped that the power unleashed by atomic energy could be used to fuel—or destroy—entire cities. Today data presents a similar tension. With newfound capabilities for targeting comes the obligation to steward the data responsibly on behalf of customers and to earn their trust with every interaction. We've all been targeted with an ad or a message that causes us to stop and think, "That was a little too personal, or maybe just creepy." Data can be used to make societies more open and free, or it can be used to subvert them by fomenting fear and hatred. It can be used to empower customers by giving them more control over their interactions with businesses, or it can be used to feed addiction and monetize baser instincts.

The first product we built at Krux in 2010 was a security offering called Data Sentry that helped web destinations detect who was skimming and stealing customer data without authorization. We believed then, as we do today, that trust and privacy are the precondition for every data-driven activity. We're proud of the commitments we made to security and trust early on and now at Salesforce, and we're encouraged that the current environment is forcing every company to come to grips with the importance of serving as a responsible steward of customer data. Without trust, every data-driven endeavor falls to pieces, which is why we'll pay special attention to how security, trust, and privacy have become so critical for the future of data-driven marketing.

At Krux we learned immensely from the people who brought their best selves to work every day and poured their energy and passion into building something great together. We also learned tremendously from our hundreds of remarkable customers, who always challenged us to turn something good into something great and to turn something great into something insanely great. What we've tried to do is distill all that toil and sweat, the losses and wins, the lessons learned, into something useful in the pages that follow.

At Krux, our ambition was always to be more than just a technology company. For so many of us, the undertaking was both an idea and an ideal, energized by shared values that went beyond products, customers, and revenue. We were privileged to build a hardworking, mega-smart team who believed in the vision of using people data to dazzle customers and who relished the many puzzles that resulted. I hope our stories inspire you to think about different ways to solve yours. Thanks for going on this journey with us.

TOM CHAVEZ
San Francisco, CA

INTRODUCTION:
THE MAGIC COFFEE MAKER

Early in 2015, we had a meeting with Keurig Green Mountain, the maker of single-serve coffee makers. The company, long considered the innovator in home brewing, had just released a brand-new version of its popular coffee maker and was in the midst of launching its new soda machine, Keurig "Kold." Like every other consumer products company, Keurig was facing fickle consumers whose tastes were harder and harder to discern, but Keurig was trying hard to innovate and establish closer relationships with its best customers—as well as find new ones.

During our meeting, without realizing it, Keurig's chief digital and information officer, Mike Cunningham, challenged us with a question that beautifully encapsulates the new normal for the modern marketer. "So, I want to put a data collection chip in our machines, but it costs about $5," he said. "Since we make tens of millions of coffee makers a year, our CFO wants to understand the value of the idea relative to its cost. Can you tell me what it's worth?"

The company wanted analytics on board the machine to understand how well it was doing its job. Was it brewing the coffee hot enough? At certain altitudes, water takes longer to get to the ideal temperature, and Keurig wanted to make sure every cup was brewed to perfection. How many K-Cups was the machine making every month? As the leading distributor of single-brew coffee capsules at retail,[1] Keurig was making more money at higher margins selling coffee than it was from selling machines. If a machine was breaking down for a 200-cup-a-month family, it would make sense to give the family another machine for free—or at least offer a heavy discount on an updated model.

Although Mike's vision for technology started with the theory that more data, and access to it, could help Keurig get closer to its buyers and provide a better customer experience, ultimately it was about achieving better performance, greater sales, or more data through a trusting relationship that respected Keurig buyers' privacy and choices. Everything else came second.

Keurig is one of the biggest retailers in the world (in the top 100 of Internet retailers), but it had no way of knowing what coffee people were brewing in its machines. While it was possible for a machine to scan proprietary K-Cups when placed in the brewer, what about third-party cups from partners? Maybe an optical scanner placed in the lid of the machine could reveal the different products being consumed—Folgers in the morning, Starbucks in the afternoon, and maybe a soothing cup of Twinings chamomile tea at night? That would give the company more direct visibility into which partners were performing well and would provide deeper insights into consumers' home brewing preferences.

Cunningham's ambitions didn't end there. What about the people brewing the coffee? Could a beacon inside the machine read the mobile devices of people in the house and find out who was brewing what? How many people were in a typical Keurig household? Survey data was great but known to be patchy and incomplete, and frequently biased toward a small sample of households. Could tying consumers through their mobile devices to other data sources help Keurig understand household income?

Was it possible to get a location on the machine and discover which local retailers had the best selection of K-Cups?

Finally, Mike dreamed of outfitting the machine with a small LCD screen. Keurig has the rapt attention of tens of millions of consumers every morning as they wait the 30 seconds for their coffee to brew.[2] Maybe the screen could suggest new brands, prompt consumers to order more when they were running low, or even serve up a video ad in exchange for a free cup of hotel coffee. In a world with connected refrigerators, the concept wasn't a stretch. Keurig was watching in-home appliance makers like Samsung lean into Internet of Things (IoT) technology to get closer to their customers alongside many other makers of home appliances.

As an astute chief data officer, Mike was asking all the right questions. How could data transform his company, bring it closer to its consumers, provide a better and more relevant coffee drinking experience, and give his team the insights it needed to compete against a sea of fast-moving competitors? It wasn't just other coffee makers they were competing with. Keurig partners with Starbucks, McDonald's, and others, but still competes for that first and last coffee of the day. Being a favored and available drink choice multiple times a day is the central imperative of beverage companies everywhere. Keurig was more agile than most with its retail partner relationships, but it still didn't have a good view of all its customers across retail.

In other words, sometimes Keurig's relationship with customers was arm's length. If a K-Cup was sold on Keurig.com or a retailer partner who shared data with the company, then there was no problem. But what about the millions of other cups sold at retail? Once Keurig sold a few cases of K-Cups to the local grocery store or hotel location, the company didn't get much access to the consumer experience. Sure, it knew how many cups it was selling, but what else were those customers filling their shopping carts with? How much did they spend at the supermarket? What was Keurig's share of basket against competitive brands? Were hotel visitors actually making a K-Cup at their hotel when they woke up, or were they waiting until they got to Dunkin' Donuts for that first cup of coffee? Also, who were the customers exactly? How much money did they have? Where did they live? What websites and apps did they spend their time on? What celebrities did they like, and what TV shows were they watching?

Mike was a trailblazer who fully imagined what Keurig could do with better access to this kind of people data from its devices. First, the company would know and understand more about the people who drink coffee at home than any other company in the world—what they drink, when they drink it, and what brands they drink. Any brand that supplied a K-Cup would seek ongoing access to that data so it could achieve deeper insights about its own customers. More important, the company would start on a journey to own more of its purchase data, especially if folks could order right from the machine or, better yet, have the machine order for them when they started to run low. This was fundamental to Mike's first principle of delighting customers through better experience delivery.

In the most basic sense, what Keurig could achieve with data, accelerated by an IoT strategy, was a sustained, truly personal relationship with its customers.

As we were growing Krux's marketer base a few years ago, we called this story "The Magic Coffee Maker" because it captured so much of what we believed: enterprises owning more of their data, the promise of connected devices and touchpoints, better consumer experiences through personalization, and the stitching together of data from many different devices to create an intelligent 360-degree profile of the consumer. Coffee makers are just one example among thousands. We're increasingly surrounded by a dizzying array of gizmos connected to the Internet: cell phones, tablets, desktop computers, TVs, gaming devices, thermometers, refrigerators, cars, and many other gadgets yet to be invented. Because of this hyperportable, pervasive connectivity that we now enjoy, the number of touchpoints that a company can use to engage with us is exploding exponentially.

More touchpoints and roughly the same number of people on the planet change the equation: *who's looking at the screen becomes more important, and much more valuable, than what's on the screen.* Every company, wherever it sits in a broader value network of partners, distributors, and customers, is trying to get closer to the person looking at the screen, or in Keurig's case, making the coffee. After years of just talk, marketers are charting data-driven strategies for delivering the right experience to the right person at the right time and the right place.

Many Internet companies recognized this challenge early and moved quickly to conquer it. They include familiar names such as Google, Facebook, and Apple and more specialized companies such as Netflix and LinkedIn. Amazon, however, stands apart in delivering the gold standard for people-centric precision. With every click and every pageview, Amazon creates a personal connection with each consumer. We feel like Amazon knows us because *it does.* Amazon uses its understanding to cross-sell and upsell, inspiring us to spend a little extra money while we are on the site, or always to think of Amazon first whenever we need a new tool, ingredient, or personal effect. And in an evolving regime where issues of privacy and data usage loom ever larger, we trust Amazon. With every return visit, we express that trust by sharing more about our wants and interests, which in turn nourishes Amazon's massive people engine with the fuel it needs to give us an even smarter, more personal touch on the next visit.

The purpose of this book, in its most basic sense, is to help you and your company channel your inner Amazon. In the pages that follow, we will help you understand the challenge of people-centric marketing in a practical way, share best practices that leading companies employ as they confront the challenge, and arm you with simple concepts and principles you can use to harness its potential for your own company and your own career. We will describe in detail the data strategies that companies such as Georgia-Pacific, Warner Bros., and Turner implemented to reinvent their relationships with consumers. We will talk about how Heineken is using data to better understand how much beer it can sell to soccer fans, how Kellogg Company uses data to save millions of dollars every year not targeting certain consumers, and how RB is working to find out when people sneeze so it can sell more Mucinex. By pioneering many of the techniques and tools in this book, dozens of trailblazers have achieved virtuosity in data-driven marketing. It gives us great confidence that you will, too.

CHAPTER 1

THE EMERGENCE OF PEOPLE DATA

Computers have been crunching data for over 60 years. The idea and the practice of data processing isn't new, so what's the big deal? We've titled this book *Data Driven*, but what do we mean exactly?

In the 1980s, enterprise resource planning systems captured data about a company's billings, bookings, backlog, and shipments.[1] Customer relationship management (CRM) systems capture data about business customers—their needs, status, and activities.[2] Internet portals in the early 2000s such as Yahoo! and MSN introduced a new twist by giving people news and information tuned to their specific interests.[3] This evolved over the last decade into a broader set of technologies for delivering more relevant ads, more effective commerce, and more customized content to people. Ticketmaster/LiveNation is using these tools to find new purchasers of Justin Bieber tickets.[4] Heineken is using them to attract new beer drinkers. When companies refer to data, they increasingly have in mind information about people: who they are, their wants, desires, needs, and expectations.

We're living in an increasingly connected world, and digital experiences—social media platforms like Twitter, online destinations like NYT.com, and mobile apps like Fandango—are the mechanism by which a brand engages with people. What differentiates this new normal from what came before is the two-way nature of the interaction. Much has been written about the old world, where you sat in your living room and watched a broadcast television show, and how different it is from the new one, in which you consume content on different screens whenever and however it suits you. What's received less attention is the data that's flowing quietly in the background as you zig and zag across screens and content. As users engage on their phones, desktops, and other touchpoints, they're leaving behind data signatures via visits, gestures, mouseovers, likes, exits, clicks, conversions, and search, all of which hold the possibility of energizing more relevant, and thus more valuable, customer experiences.

This "people data," the distinctive digital signatures that people leave behind when they interact with the connected digital world,[5] permeates virtually every nook and cranny of our day-to-day lives. It resides in an invisible fabric—quiet, electric, always on. When collected and organized the right way, it offers powerful signals about who we really are, what we like, what we hate, who we want to become. Capturing, organizing, and acting on it defines the new basis of competition in marketing and will separate the winners from the losers for years to come.

Before delving into what's to come, though, we first need a deeper understanding of this invisible data fabric. Where does people data come from? How is it generated? Who captures and uses it?

It all began with Internet advertising.

INTERNET ADVERTISING:
A BRIEF, OVERSIMPLIFIED HISTORY

In the very early days of Internet advertising, media buyers working for Nike, which wanted more consumers to buy its shoes, would pick up the phone and call Yahoo!, MSN, or AOL salespeople to buy banner ads in the sports section. Just like television and radio, the media buy was transacted through something called an "insertion order" (which is just the media industry's name for a purchase order), and the price and volume of the package were negotiated manually. Yahoo! would run the banner ads to the broad range of visitors to the sports section and provide reporting on the performance and pacing of the campaign. Most sites, whether stand-alone sites like iVillage or channels within the major portals, were based on demographic composition and audience penetration: moms could be found on mom sites, auto intenders on car sites, businesspeople on news sites, etc. It was just like television, except that marketers could get a more precise sense of how things were working by studying the ad delivery and campaign reports that Yahoo!, AOL, and MSN gave them. In the beginning, they could see the number of impressions and clicks generated by their ads; over time, the reports were enriched to give them additional information such as location and time of day.

The mid- to late 1990s were heady times for digital advertisers. Early browsers such as Netscape, Mosaic, and Microsoft demonstrated the openness and dynamism of the Internet by their very design. By marshaling information from virtually any source, immediately delivering a page to dazzle you, and then rinse-wash-repeating whenever you decided to click again, they made the limitlessness of the new digital age apparent to even the most skeptical users. While individual people have their favorite browser, a cool feature of Internet Explorer is that if you look at the bottom left as a page is rendered, you see a fast-moving array of activities representing all the calls the browser is making to external sources to render your page that very moment. While you might not be aware of it, behind the scenes a complicated symphony is unfolding wherein your device calls out to the web, receives content, and organizes it in real time into a page just for you.

Data about who was looking at the screen was captured via little pieces of code called "cookies," which were invented by Marc Andreessen and his team during the development of the Mosaic browser in 1993.[6] Cookies were a way for websites to store a little bit of information about the person who was using the browser, initially with the objective of helping your browser remember what you put in your cart while you were shopping. Through the use of cookies and the code that sets and references cookies in a browser (referred to interchangeably as "pixels," "tags," or "beacons"), websites gained the ability to identify and track specific users across the Internet. Importantly, they can't identify you individually; you appear in one of their systems as a piece of gobbledygook (e.g., cookie-ID FGc397e4k), akin to the inscrutable serial numbers you encounter when you try to register a new mobile phone or TV.

The activity that's happening while you surf the web on a browser is, via cookies, decoupled completely from whatever content is published on the page itself. It is also made visible to those external sources that your browser calls out to as it assembles your page. In the early 2000s, many of those external sources began to accumulate troves of cookies with information, such as the URL of the website you had last visited, and they leveraged this information to conduct a kind of bare-bones contextual segmentation. Go to http//www.univision.com, and you could reliably be identified as a Spanish speaker. Accessing http://www.wsj.com makes you a business news reader, and checking http://www.espn.com pegs you as a sports enthusiast. The hierarchical organization of a website provided a natural way to further fine-tune your profile. For example, a visit to http://www.espn.com/NBA/ establishes you not just as a sports enthusiast but as a professional basketball fan, while a visit to http://www.espn.com/NFL/ marks you as a professional football fan.

As the unbinding of media from data became more broadly understood, a new species emerged from the primordial digital soup: the ad network. Stand-alone ad networks with names like AdMagnet, AdForm, AdBrite, and Blue Lithium exploited this decoupling of people data from content and media to build fast-growing advertising services that gave marketers the ability to reach an apparently infinite number of segments. Networks helped publishers by bundling their inventory and selling it in packages that extended marketers' reach across very specific audiences. Hyperprecision, or at least the promise of it, became the calling card for a fast-growing sector of intermediaries in the global $1 trillion advertising industry.

Marketers loved it. They began to issue requests for proposals with strange, increasingly obsessive-compulsive demands like, "Find me 250,000 moms in Albuquerque with a propensity to purchase cream cheese for baking, not bagels." For the first time, they could separate the people they wanted to reach from the media properties they visited. "Auto intenders" could be found not just on Cars.com but on thousands of entertainment and news sites. Car manufacturers loved buying "auto intenders" on the cheap, without having to pay big premiums for specialty-site buys—and the news and entertainment sites got new sources of revenue as the networks dug out all kinds of specialty audiences from their properties and leveraged their sales forces to extract media buys from agencies.

Networks enjoyed a business model based essentially on arbitrage. They could buy plain-vanilla, untargeted users for $2 CPM from publishers that were experiencing surges in traffic much larger than what they could monetize with their own sales teams; curate and package those users into more valuable audience packages using cookies and contextual segmentation; and deliver $20 "travel intenders" on the other side. Hundreds of new ad networks sprouted overnight, and millions of pixels and tags were deployed on publisher sites to track the world's Internet surfers.

Very soon thereafter, a new innovation took root: the ability not only to buy audiences separately from the media, but to buy them in real time via a system that resembled the stock market. Real-time bidding, also known as "programmatic media," gave media buyers the ability to bid on people's attention and to value each ad impression individually. Instead of having to buy millions of advertising impressions at a fixed rate, media buyers could instruct these systems to find users based on their willingness to pay. Auto marketers would enter bids of "up to $8" against their competitors for users who looked like "auto intenders." Sometimes they would pay the full price, but often they could "win" users for much less. The innovation of real-time bidding created what we now think of as programmatic marketing—the ability of machines to listen to the content experiences of billions of people on the Internet and to serve them an ad at the very moment they visit a website or mobile app, according to prespecified bidding conditions.

Programmatic media took a lot of power from publishers and placed it directly with the marketer's "trading desk," agency folks trained to use algorithms to sort through advertising exchanges and find the right people as cheaply as possible. It also demolished the ad network's central value proposition—the curation and packaging of ad inventory from publishers—by turning it into a fully automated, machine-driven, real-time process. Before trading desks came along, agencies relied on ad networks to do the programmatic buying for them. The agencies got smart quickly and realized that all they had to do to leverage their massive buying power was to own the technology and teams to buy media in this new environment. Instead of publishers or ad networks making fat profit margins from arbitraging media, agency trading desks became the intermediaries buying low and selling high. Soon, every agency created its own proprietary trading desk, and hundreds of millions of dollars in digital advertising began to flow through the agencies.

These developments were a mixed bag for marketers. Sure, more performance data was flowing, and media prices seemed to be decreasing thanks to technology that effectively treated Internet surfers like pork bellies traded in a commodities market— but the promised cost efficiencies remained elusive. After all the technology fees paid to the many intermediaries between marketers and publishers, marketers were seeing very little improvement in reach for every dollar spent.

The battle for access to consumer audiences over the last 20 years is thus marked by the rise and fall of different players vying for control and scale. Initially, publishers owned the relationship with audiences and carefully protected external access to them. As more people flocked to the Internet, publishers couldn't hire enough salespeople to peddle all the available impressions. Networks helped publishers by packaging the inventory they couldn't sell themselves, and briefly owned the power to reach people at scale. Then the trading desks came in, promising marketers programmatic access to people in real time. The net effect has been for both publishers and marketers to move further and further away from their audiences and become more dependent upon technology intermediaries to broker the connection between marketers and the people they want to reach. Except for mammoth publishers such as Google and Facebook—both propelled more by technology than content—most publishers are struggling as their share of advertising revenue erodes and the costs of innovation soar ever higher.

As digital media evolved between 1995 and 2015, most marketers took a wait-and-see approach, relying on their agencies to buy the new Internet ad formats alongside traditional television, print, and radio placements. But a few pioneers got into the game early, took risks, and never stopped learning. For Warner Bros., Internet advertising was never an end state, but rather a stopping point in a broader, multiyear push to reinvent the way it engages with consumers. Its experience offers a powerful vignette of the evolution of digital media from the perspective of a modern marketer.

CASE IN POINT

Warner Bros. Leverages Digital Media and Data to Redefine Its Relationship with Consumers

Launched in 1923, Warner Bros. is one of the most successful, storied movie studios in Hollywood.[7] For decades it focused on conceiving, green-lighting, and producing action movies like *Wonder Woman*, dramas like *The Blind Side*, and family entertainment like *The Lego Movie*.[8] The rhythm and flow of Warner Bros.' business was steady and unchanging: produce a movie; market it on billboards and TV; distribute it through theater chains like AMC[9]; collect revenue from ticket sales; repeat. Starting in 1999, key changes began that would forever upend the formula that Warner Bros. had used for nearly 60 years.

Consumers were going to new web portals like Yahoo! and MSN to read reviews and early posts from other consumers who were buzzing about a new movie. The balance of power shifted. Suddenly, thousands of consumers online had the audacity to do Siskel and Ebert's job for them, posting their own thoughts and reviews on chat sites and other online movie forums. Anecdotes began to proliferate regarding Yahoo!'s ability to predict box office sales, based on the number of pageviews and postings that people saw in connection with the launch of a new movie. Warner Bros. and its competitors rapidly extended their traditional marketing mix of TV, magazines, and billboards to include the

(continued)

purchase of ads on portal sites. While this proved useful, it felt to Warner Bros. executives like they were simply taking existing offline marketing methods and grafting them onto the online channel. When Warner Bros. received reports from the portals regarding who saw the ads it was buying, the company began to understand that online marketing offered possibilities for precision targeting and customer insights not achievable with print, billboards, or TV.

"You have to understand, every time we launched a new action movie, while the Theatrical marketing team executed brilliant creative and marketing strategy, they were forced to use a playbook without direct visibility into which consumers go to action movies and those who are only interested in romantic comedies," says Justin Herz, executive vice president of digital product, platform, and strategy. "It wasn't done that way because we were lazy. It was because we couldn't see or interact directly with the people buying movie tickets. Distributors had always been between us and our end consumers. But the web started to change this dynamic for us in a pretty fundamental way."

Using actual ticket delivery and purchase information, Warner Bros. started to build verifiable hypotheses about people with a propensity to purchase an action movie ticket. For the first time, it could see the age, geography, and gender of the people who were viewing and clicking on the company's content—a tectonic shift for Warner Bros.' marketing department. Recognizing the possibilities, the company took the unusual move of buying a web media property, Flixster, in 2011,[10] not because Warner Bros. wanted to get into the web media game, but because it saw the value of the data that Flixster was generating about what movies consumers liked, what movies they hated, and (most important) why.

As new online channels and touchpoints took root and as Warner Bros. deepened its base of experience via investments like Flixster and new infrastructure for securely leveraging consumer data, while maintaining the consumer's privacy, the company achieved a new intimacy with the people buying its movie tickets. "We understand consumers in a much more detailed way, and this has allowed us to navigate an incredibly intense shift in media and content consumption by our consumers over the last decade," says Herz.

Flixster data unlocked new insights that supercharged Warner Bros. marketing, giving it direct access to all kinds of real-time data about people, the types of movies they watch, where they watch them, and how many they watch. As a subsidiary of Time Warner, Warner Bros. can also collaborate with sister companies, such as HBO, to find audiences across both fan bases. Before it undertook a people data marketing strategy, taking a "no-brainer" approach such as marketing *Creed* to fans of HBO boxing was impossible.

Today, securely sharing data across your organization is no longer impossible. It is a necessity, and companies that cannot take advantage of cross-organizational data synergies are vulnerable to disruption.[11] We'll share tools

(continued)

to help your company execute cross-functional data strategies in Chapter 5.

LOOMING THREATS: CONSUMER PRIVACY AND SECURITY

Digital experiences beget data. Data begets more valuable experiences. Savvy companies like Warner Bros. are exploiting this virtuous circle to improve revenue and deepen relationships with customers.

As an asset, data possesses several unique, powerful qualities. First, it follows an important law from information economics: its marginal cost is zero, which means that once it exists, it can be put to possibly thousands or millions of potential uses without wear or tear. Data doesn't complain and rarely gets sick. Unlike an ad, it doesn't consume valuable real estate on a screen or a billboard. Its delivery and opportunity costs are nearly zero. As big data infrastructure from companies like Amazon, Microsoft, and Google takes root, the unit costs of capturing and processing it continue to fall year-over-year at astonishing rates.

The cost, abundance, and durability characteristics of people data sound too good to be true. As with all breakthroughs, however, with great possibility comes potential peril. With data, the greatest risks center on privacy, security, and trust.

The "great unbinding" of people data from content, as we have observed, gave rise to new tools such as real-time bidding and new players such as ad networks. With cookies and tracking pixels, ad networks and agencies could identify and track specific users across the Internet, but this capability had a dark side. Networks could use those same tracking techniques to gain backdoor access to valuable user information without the website operator's knowledge or authorization, resulting in what we called "data leakage" in a 2010 post.[12] The dangers were real: first, for the media publishers that had invested so heavily to create the content that attracted users initially, but also for end users who were becoming increasingly irritated by being chased all across the Internet with the same shoe ad after looking at a stylish pair just once on one of their favorite sites.

Let's take the *Wall Street Journal* as an example. When an advertiser, or more likely its agency or ad network partner, runs an ad on http://www.wsj.com, it can quietly drop a pixel into the ad and use that little piece of code to set a cookie on the user. If the user was in the Finance section reading a page about fixed income securities, for example, the reader could be placed in a "Wall Street Journal—Fixed Income" segment. If an advertiser or ad network wants to engage with that user again, it would take the data it acquired in this fashion and use it to target the user on other sites, but with ad slots that are much cheaper than the *WSJ*. Effectively, it uses the *WSJ* user data to bypass *WSJ* altogether, even though *WSJ* did all the heavy lifting to create the article about municipal bonds that brought the user to the website in the first place. In the realm of music, when a songwriter writes a song, he or she earns royalties every time that song is performed. If songwriting were like digital publishing circa 2010, the songwriter could write a great song and watch someone else perform it in stadiums, radio, and TV, over and over again, without earning a penny from the effort.

Media publishers tried to stem this data leakage by ceasing ad sales to ad networks and insisting that advertisers come and buy from them directly. But the genie was out of the bottle. Getting him back in required attention to questions of data security: Which players were getting their code onto the websites via ads or other means? How much data were they collecting, and about which users? Was this a one-off phenomenon, or was it a trend? In 2010, we conducted a study at Krux that showed how pervasive data skimming and theft were across verticals, segments, and sectors. Across the top 50 publishers included in our study, we found that:

- Thirty-one percent of all data collection was initiated by entities other than the publishers themselves, demonstrating how little control publishers wielded in governing data collection practices on their own sites.

- Fifty-five percent of all data collectors were using standard technical methods to usher in at least one other data collector behind them. The pirates weren't showing up alone; they were bringing friends.

- Twenty-eight percent of the total volume of data collection events clustered around entities such as ad networks and newer variants called demand-side platforms and real-time exchanges, reflecting considerable growth in data collection for companies that barely existed just a few years ago.

- One hundred sixty-seven external companies were observed collecting data from the 50 publishers in our study, underscoring the intensity with which intermediaries were going after publishers with valuable people data.

As intermediaries continued to pump digital experiences for data, the drums began to beat on matters of privacy and consumer trust. Beginning in 2012 a notable shift in policy and market sentiment took root, as many started to question the provenance of the data being used to fuel customer experiences. Smart marketers and publishers started to take more seriously the challenge of navigating an evolving privacy regime. "At Kellogg's, we knew that responsible stewardship of our consumer data was a strategic imperative," says Jon Suarez-Davis, who was head of digital marketing at Kellogg's at the time. "We saw the toll Target's data breach in 2015 took, and it awakened a new urgency to shore up our policies, practices, and technologies. Good data governance went from being something looked at occasionally to something that our CEO and Board were determined to nail."[13]

The digital economy is built on the interplay between convenience and privacy. Consumers implicitly recognize that advertising is essential for free or low-cost access to a huge array of content, services, and apps. At the same time, they resent feeling as if Big Brother is watching them—and therein lies the rub.

The tension between privacy and personalization runs deep, increasing in urgency every time a new technology for capturing people data gains traction. While the regulatory bodies of many nations, including the United States, take a relatively lax approach to consumer privacy, the European Union imposes exacting guidelines for the handling of personal data and stiff penalties for failing to meet them. At the time of this writing, EU privacy regulations appear unignorable for U.S. businesses simply because so many of them interact with EU citizens over web- or app-enabled experiences. For this reason it's impossible to make sense of consumer trust, security, and privacy without gaining a practical understanding of the origins and status of EU privacy regulations.

EUROPEAN PRIVACY REGULATIONS: A TEMPLATE FOR MANAGING CONSUMER PRIVACY

In the European Union, local and regional regulatory bodies negotiate fiercely with businesses on behalf of consumer privacy in a tense, never-ending game of tug-and-pull. In 2000, a transatlantic pact called EU Safe Harbor was negotiated between regulatory bodies in Europe and the United States that allowed companies to move digital information to the United States from Europe. The agreement established rules of the road, ensuring that data collected from EU citizens and transferred to the United States for further processing was safeguarded by U.S. companies under the more stringent EU framework. In essence, Safe Harbor made it possible for everyone from Google and Facebook to once-small start-ups like Uber to operate freely in Europe, provided they adhered to the framework.

Edward Snowden threw a match on dry tinder in 2013 when he revealed the extent to which the U.S. National Security Agency was collecting information on public and private citizens worldwide. Soon thereafter, negotiations for a new Safe Harbor agreement began in earnest. Many of the issues exposed by Snowden became sticking points in the final negotiations of a new agreement. With the United States and the European Union unable to agree on a new arrangement, in mid-October 2016 Europe's highest court annulled the Safe Harbor pact, effectively returning authority over data collection practices to local regulators across EU member states.[14, 15]

There was a widespread misconception that the EU Safe Harbor ruling would spell the immediate end of normal business dealings. This proved not to be the case, and it points to a larger trend where pessimists foretell the complete upending of digital businesses in response to a pending policy or regulatory pronouncement, always followed by a softening period during which regulators and businesses agree to meet somewhere in the middle. Soon after the EU ruling, both sides of the Atlantic issued statements that an "agreement in principle" for a new Safe Harbor[16] had been reached and that all parties, including the U.S. Senate, had until February 1, 2016, to ratify it.[17]

A brief limbo ensued. Companies fell back to a complex web of legal agreements that document the what-how-why of their work for each company and in each EU country where they do business. The European Union provided for this fallback scenario via the so-called Model Clauses or Model Contract Clauses. In essence, Model Clauses were adjuncts to existing commercial agreements, officially sanctioned and generally recognized and accepted by EU and local regulatory agencies. They served to outline which data is transferred and for which purposes, they confirmed that both parties agree to it, and they provided assurances that such data transfers adhere to all relevant data protection requirements.

The problem with Model Clauses was that they failed to provide a global, "adopt once–apply everywhere" approach that consumer-facing companies could depend on to unify and manage their data practices. All affected companies needed to adhere to multiple, country-specific standards rather than a single set of

EU-wide rules. The complexity resulting from different rules in effect across the European Union was significant, starting with the most basic definition of personal data. Germany, for example, considers the IP address (the code the Internet assigns the on-ramp you use to go online) of individual users as personal information that could not be used for tracking or targeting; other countries do not. Beyond spawning a compliance nightmare, it was oddly dissonant with the European Union's raison d'être: to promote frictionless commerce among companies and consumers freely across borders.

A resolution came in the form of an EU-wide arrangement called Global Data Protection Regulation (GDPR) in April 2016, and the law took effect in May 2018.[18] GDPR first mandates a "right to be forgotten," essentially, a consumer's right to be deleted from any system that tracks him or her. While its implementation is fairly well understood, there are a number of what engineers call "edge conditions" that require more clarification as of the time of this writing. For example, does the cookie "FGc397e4k" corresponding to just one of the multiple devices you own fall under the jurisdiction of GDPR? Is it you in totality that is to be forgotten, or you on just this particular browser that the regulation covers? Suppose a U.S. citizen travels to the EU and visits a local website to make a dinner reservation, and suppose in that context the reservation website sets a cookie. Is it an EU cookie? If the user asks to be deleted, how does the website discern whether the owner of the browser is an EU citizen or a U.S. citizen?

So in a lizard-eating-its-tail kind of irony, there are cases where the right to be forgotten outstrips the capabilities of the underlying technologies it is intended to govern. Like any regulation, it specifies the ends without determining the means and leaves the implementation, as well as the interpretation of its compliance, to regulators. Its principal thrust, to give consumers control over whether they can be tracked, remains a necessary pillar of any complete framework for consumer privacy. Systems like the ones we've built at Krux, when architected properly, give their adopters the confidence to operate flexibly as edge conditions get sorted out in practice.

GDPR further promotes (but does not explicitly insist on) a consent requirement: every company is to clearly disclose in plain language what it is doing with an individual's personal data and every way it plans to use the data. Moreover, it must obtain consent to use that personal data *before* it engages with the user. If the user does not consent, the company cannot refuse to deliver services.

The consent requirement poses a conundrum for any publisher on the other side of the screen investing millions of dollars in compelling content for consumers. Whether consumers explicitly recognize the ad model that underpins their free access to content, we worry whether it's feasible to presume that free content will continue to flow if consumers opt out but with a guarantee of continued access for free. Either governments will have to step in to subsidize content creation themselves, or a more tenable deal will need to be struck, one that allows the purveyors of digital experiences to stay afloat and earn a profit. For publishers suffering from steadily declining revenue and market share over the last decade, this aspect of GDPR presents an especially acute problem. It's one we don't claim to know how to solve. At the time of this writing, European publishers continue to struggle with GDPR compliance, and Google's publisher business has limited its pool of approved "third-party" partners, resulting in steep revenue declines for many small to mid-sized digital publishers.[19]

A final twist in GDPR is called the "right to explanation," which stipulates that EU citizens can contest "legal or similarly significant" decisions made by algorithms and appeal for human intervention. Articles 21 and 22 of GDPR introduce the principle that people are owed agency and understanding when they're faced by machine-made decisions. If AI-driven marketing systems, which we will cover in subsequent chapters, give you an answer you don't like or present you with an offer you find insulting or irrelevant, you have the right to have the system that sent the message explain itself. More specifically, you can demand that the *company* that uses the system that generated the undesirable message explain why its system performed as it did.

Plainly, there is still much to be sorted when it comes to navigating the line between convenience and privacy for consumers inside and outside the EU. The success of our future business models and regulatory frameworks hinges on the degree to which they can respond to unintended consequences and gracefully absorb future shocks. Without question, the best example of such a shock is the Facebook–Cambridge Analytica episode of 2018. Benjamin Franklin once wrote that "pain is instructive"—which is why it's productive for us to turn our attention to it now.

CASE IN POINT

The Facebook–Cambridge Analytica Debacle

Too much of the reporting about Facebook and Cambridge Analytica was sensationalistic, which resulted in too many unfortunate misconceptions. The narrative you likely read is that a sketchy U.K. company called Cambridge Analytica, with the help of a pink-haired, nose-ringed technical wunderkind named Chris Wylie, "hacked" Facebook and stole 50 million user profiles. The company weaponized the data and used it to psychologically manipulate British citizens to vote in favor of Brexit and U.S. voters to elect Donald Trump president of the United States. It was the gravest security breach since the North Korean cyberattack on Sony's e-mail systems in late 2014.

The reality is a lot more pedestrian.

There was no hack. There was no breach. Cambridge Analytica used a feature freely provided by Facebook in the plain light of day; the company did not exploit a bug or a backdoor. The scary part was that it was a capability available to all developers across the planet for years, and which tens of thousands used.

In the interest of keeping focus and avoiding tangents, we will set aside the question of whether the kind of psychographic targeting Cambridge Analytica was attempting to perform even works and whether it tilted the U.K. or U.S. elections in any way. We also lay aside the question of whether Facebook is liable, as in "the doctor left a pair of scissors inside a patient and was found liable for damages." As Mark Zuckerberg affirmed before Congress in April 2018, Facebook was certainly *responsible* for the decisions it made, which led to the outcomes achieved by Cambridge Analytica (and many more companies that are likely still to surface).   *(continued)*

How did this happen?

On April 21, 2010, Facebook launched the first version of its Graph API. API stands for "application programming interface." It's a tool that computer scientists use to get computers to talk to each other. In essence, it specifies a syntax by which information can move between two systems and actions that an authorized system can instruct another to take (for example, "get me all users who live in Minnesota, are hockey fans, and have a college degree"). Facebook closed its Graph API on April 30, 2015. During the previous *five years*, virtually any developer could programmatically harness a torrent of user information, which was scraped from Facebook profiles after users granted permission for third-party apps to access their data. You've seen the confirmation window that pops up when someone wants to play a game or use Facebook to log in, rather than create a new password for a new site? That's the gateway, the little moment of truth so many people skip over, that fueled the data for Facebook's Graph API.

A University of Cambridge academic named Aleksandr Kogan created a "Test Your Personality" app and used the Graph API to harvest profile data on 270,000 users. As in the New Testament, where a few loaves and fish are multiplied to feed a crowd of thousands, 270,000 was turned into *50 million* profiles by leveraging another Facebook feature that enabled developers to access the profiles of not just the person who installed an app, but all the person's friends as well. The permission for this was buried in a mostly ignored section deep in your Facebook settings, which privacy groups tried to call attention to for years without success.[20] Kogan's amplification of 270,000 profiles into 50 million wasn't a hack, an exploit, or the leveraging of a bug; it was the use of a feature that was widely available and openly published as part of the Facebook Graph API. He sold the data to Cambridge Analytica—which was indeed a breach of Facebook's data-sharing policies—but certainly not a breach in the systems security sense of the word.

Later, in 2015, Facebook discovered that the data transfer from Kogan to Cambridge Analytica had occurred, asked for written confirmation that the data had been deleted, and considered the matter closed. Remember, there were tens of thousands of developers harvesting data in this way. Once the data left Facebook's servers, it vanished untraceably into the ether. There was simply no way to know where it went and how it was used. This makes it hard, or just impossible, to prove occurrence, harm, or damage from the misuse of the data. We should be unfazed, however, if and when whistle-blowing revelations about a black market for Facebook data, captured and traded by external developers between 2010 and 2015, come to light.

Ultimately, Facebook recognized the problems with the architecture of its first implementation of its Graph API and changed the policy in 2015. Since those revelations of misuse, Facebook has been attempting to clean up the mess and rebuild trust with users.

The data that Facebook has collected (or that consumers have unknowingly handed over for free) seems unfathomably huge. While it *is* impressive, it will seem adorably inconsequential relative to the jungles and forests of unconquered new terrain soon to flourish in the next 15 years. Every machine experience, every human experience, is getting turned into data at a rate that even Google, Facebook, and Amazon will struggle to control, and that will give rise to new technologies and new companies yet to be launched.

THE DATAFICATION OF EVERYTHING

Big data technologies allow us to capture, store, and process increasingly vast amounts of information. In 2000, less than one-quarter of the world's information was in digital form. Today less than 2 percent of the world's information is nondigital, macro evidence of profound, lightning-fast change.

Given its massive scale, it's tempting to understand big data just in terms of storage, but that misses the big picture. First, we don't just capture and store ever-larger sources of information. We crunch and compute the information at rising velocity. We send instructions to your browser, the Pandora station in your car, and your coffee maker to give you more of what you want at every moment. Second, and more powerful, big data gives us the capability to turn every aspect of our everyday experience into data. Location is turned into data via latitude-longitude pairs phoned in from GPS satellites. LinkedIn turns professional connections into data. Facebook turns preferences and profiles into data. Google turns affinities and curiosities into data via search queries.

This process of turning every aspect of everyday life into data, *datafication*, isn't the same as digitization. Digitization takes analog information—music, books, photographs—and turns it into a string of 1s and 0s. Datafication is broader and far deeper, and there are virtually no remaining parts of our experience that are immune to its effects. Its possibilities range from the sublime to the pedestrian.

An interesting example of datafication comes to us from Professor Shigeomi Koshimizu at the Advanced Institute of Industrial Technology in Tokyo. Professor Koshimizu has devised a method for recording the contours of your body, your posture, and your weight distribution and turning this information into a personal data signature that's unique to just you. His system identifies individuals according to how they sit in a chair, on a bench, on a couch, on any surface. And it does so with 98 percent accuracy.[21] So there you have it; in a future that's hurtling toward us faster than we might like, even your posterior can be datafied.

The technology might seem silly at first blush, but its implications are potentially far-reaching. The most immediate application is in antitheft systems for cars. If you step into a car equipped with Koshimizu's system and your derriere isn't recognized, the car could demand a password before allowing you to start it. High-end luxury cars allow you to customize the height, lumbar support, and angle of your seat; why not use Koshimizu's data signature to customize your sitting experiences during all the other hours of your day? A chair powered by Koshimizu's technology could increase or reduce the lumbar support it provides based on who's in the chair, just like Keurig's coffee maker might give dad a stronger cup of Sumatra first thing in the morning while saving the medium-roast French hazelnut for mom a little later when she's getting the kids to school.

Sitting is a basic human activity ripe for personalization, and Koshimizu's technology holds the keys to transforming it. But it's just one of thousands. As new objects and experiences become datafied, they give rise to large arrays of new data signatures that need to get mapped to just you. And this is why the modern marketer needs to become comfortable with the multiplicity of you, the reality that there is no one key, no single thumbprint, that adequately reflects who you are.

IDENTITY: THE MULTIPLE VERSIONS OF YOU

Identity in the new regime is about seeing and managing the multiple versions of you. Sophisticated new technologies can be used to identify you through online cookies, mobile phone identifiers, e-mail addresses, and various device IDs and keys such as Koshimizu's. But at the end of the day, devices and browsers don't buy or engage with a brand—people do. In 2016, people owned an average of 3.64 devices per person,[22] and it is estimated that, by 2020, the number will go up to 4.3.[23] We think it will be a lot higher.

If you've heard about "browser marketing" or "mobile marketing," it's important to recognize them as a start, but they're not the whole picture. Through interactions with their mobile phones, tablets, laptops, desktops, and other connected devices (watches, toasters, chairs, cars), people create 2.5 exabytes of data every single day.[24] That is the equivalent of the content of 250,000 Libraries of Congress. Very little of that data is collected, much less analyzed. Even less of it is tied together in a single system and mapped to a real person.

Every signal that individual consumers generate can be used to understand more about who they are, what they like, and what they hate. To make sense of those signals and to make them actionable, however, we need to collect them in a single system somehow and map them to a single person. As an example, let's think about some of the data signals we might be able to collect over several weeks or months from a car shopper and what it might mean to the auto marketer trying to reach her. Table 1.1 depicts the scenario.

Table 1.1 **The Multiple Versions of a Car Shopper and the Valuable Signals She Leaves**

Action	Data Signal	Device	What the Data Means
Viewed cable ad for minivan	Ad view	MVPD (cable box)	Saw a spot for the new 2018 model minivan
Liked minivan page	Social affinity	App interaction on mobile phone	Probably a parent. Likely in market for a car
Viewed minivan page	Pageview	Browser on tablet	Has intent to purchase
Read minivan review	Pageview	Browser on desktop	In market soon for a minivan
Clicked on "credit application"	Click	Different browser on desktop	Really, really in market for that minivan!
Went into showroom	Beacon	Mobile/IoT	Person is a local retail buyer
Went into another showroom	E-mail capture	Offline/CRM	A competitive shopper and will visit dealers within a certain distance of home
Signed up for a quote	E-mail	Offline	Actively in purchase mode
Watched 30 online video ads on luxury model	Video completion	Browser	Purchase consideration; upsell opportunity
Bought the minivan at the dealer location	Offline purchase	Point of sale	New customer! Journey complete!

This sequence of events happens thousands of times every month as people in the market for a new family car go through the process. Viewed together, this makes complete sense and describes the experience of a parent researching the family's new car.

But nobody ever sees this summary.

Even though this type of customer journey happens all the time, and auto marketers know these steps result in the sale of a car, the auto marketers never get to see the journey in full resolution. Social data stays on the social platform. The fact that the buyer registered her e-mail on the dealer's CRM never connected to the buyer. And the online display advertising data is reported through an interface or spreadsheet separately from the video advertising data. Those different actions are never tied back to a single person—the mom with the mobile phone, desktop computer, e-mail address, cable box, coffee maker, or posterior-sensing couch. If we could somehow collect all this data, time-stamp every interaction, and tie it to a real person, we might have a chance of customizing a better experience, knowing what offer to present or what color to make the minivan the next time she visits the website. These are puzzles and possibilities we'll be exploring in depth in the chapters that follow.

OPERATING IN A DATAFIED WORLD WITH TRUST AND TRANSPARENCY

For the modern marketer, the datafication of everything leads to more and more versions of you, which compounds the complexity—and the urgency—of managing privacy and trust. Few have considered the implications to the personal data landscape that will come from connected cars and wearables, or things as straightforward as Keurig's coffee maker or Koshimizu's couch. The FTC is wrestling with the implications[25] of the Internet of Things (IoT) and the massive data flow that's to come.[26] Appropriately, it is calling for proactive investments from the enterprises in data security, just as it is ironing out sensible regulatory frameworks to govern the commercial activity and deep consumer engagement that will come from widespread IoT connectivity.

The practitioner's best hope of navigating an evolving privacy regime is to follow a fourfold path:

1. **Engage with policy makers.** Policy makers need help. Business operators have a vested interest in honoring consumer privacy and preventing invasive business practices. Policies drafted in a vacuum can often lead to irrational outcomes and unintended consequences. CMOs especially need to make their voices heard in advancing strategies and resolutions that strike a healthy balance between consumer privacy and business viability.

2. **Hire a top-notch privacy counsel.** Privacy policies can get extremely abstract. Barebones, unsophisticated efforts to comply can overshoot the mark, overwhelm your technical staff, and possibly ruin your business. Difficult decisions about where to draw the line are certainly ahead. A well-informed, practically minded privacy counsel who can authentically balance business interests, technical considerations, and consumer privacy concerns is a scarce but hugely precious hire.

3. **Drive organizational alignment.** Compliance with privacy policy requires a delicate balance among business

needs, technical constraints, and legal imperatives. It is, moreover, not just something lawyers do; it is a collection of practices and processes enabled by technology to which operators must adhere. The CMO's objective should be to situate herself at the center of the dialogue and to establish role definitions and incentive architectures that reliably move the organization to a sensible equilibrium point on compliance. We will delve deeper into these aspects in Chapter 6.

4. **Operate with trust and transparency.** Above all, trust and transparency.

For any company seeking to create durable, trusting experiences with consumers in the years ahead, the Facebook–Cambridge Analytica episode underscores the importance of trust and transparency. Data harvesting from Facebook unfolded behind a veil of technical abstruseness understood by software developers but very few others. The tools for data collection were recorded in manuals that only techies read, and the privacy controls were buried deep inside Facebook's user settings. Most users skipped the settings in their zeal to check their feed and see what their friends were doing, which underscores the importance of designing experiences that require consumers to stop and pay a few seconds of attention to issues that might otherwise seem dreary and uninteresting. In this dimension, GDPR's right to consent provides a valuable starting point for changing the conversation with consumers.

Stewardship of consumer data is a heavy trust. Companies that do it well will resist the urge to hide behind lawyerly terms of service or policies with legalese that average consumers struggle to understand. They'll make sure that privacy controls for users are clearly explained and easily accessible. On Krux's website, we posted a privacy policy, which met the necessary legal standards that our corporate lawyers wanted to see in place. Separately, we posted a "privacy promise," which explained in laypeople's terms what we were doing with data on behalf of our customers and what we viewed to be acceptable, proper applications of data inside our systems, irrespective of whether they were strictly legal or even discoverable. We made it clear that we would cease to do business with our own customers if we learned they were flouting any of these promises. Given the extreme volume of precious people data we were handling, it was important, we felt, to be as transparent as possible about these otherwise arcane matters.

Years later, when we first began partnership conversations with Salesforce (long before we were acquired), we were encouraged to learn that Salesforce espouses trust, broadly encompassing all practices governing its relationships with customers, as its number one principle. After we became part of Salesforce, we were further delighted to see that trust wasn't merely an idea that was paid lip service in marketing and conference materials, but an operating principle that permeated every aspect of the business. While there are always moments when we need to unpack what trust requires at a more granular level when we're deep inside the guts of a technical puzzle, all employees intuitively grasp what it means—and the clarity of thinking and the goodwill it engenders lead to durable, aboveboard relationships with all our partners and customers.

Marketers who prioritize trust and transparency with their own clients and partners, particularly when it comes to handling precious people data, reap meaningful rewards in positive perception and brand equity over the long term. They nurture deeper, more durable bonds with customers. And in a world where everything is becoming datafied at blinding speed, they substantially reduce the odds of future data breaches and hacks with brand-killing potential.

THREE CORE PRINCIPLES FOR BUILDING A WINNING DATA STRATEGY

Now that you are armed with an understanding of the data landscape, it's time to give you three core principles that encapsulate most of what we've learned during a decade immersed in data. Master them early, and you can avoid the ratholes we and others have been down where we can promise, no cheese awaits you. We offer them with a view toward helping you break old habits. If you're already a successful data-driven marketer, they can help clarify what you have already intuited but perhaps haven't yet consciously confirmed. Taken together, we believe they offer a sound framework for crafting durable data strategies and steering your organization and your career toward a more successful approach to modern marketing.

PRINCIPLE #1: EMBRACE THE HUMAN BECOMING

Heraclitus, a Greek philosopher, wrote that you can never step into the same river twice. His idea was that the only constant in the universe is change, an especially apt notion for the modern marketer seeking to make sense of the behavior of fast-moving, unpredictable consumers. It requires the unlearning, however, of two closely held precepts: the segment and the funnel.

Marketers learn the concept of a segment early in their career. Usually, this takes the form of a demographic (for example, males 18–34 years old) or a category of people with shared behavior (soup buyers, allergy sufferers, auto intenders, soccer moms). Alan Cooper, a San Francisco–based software designer, is largely credited for doing the first serious work on persona development in the 1970s.[1] We have been segmenting users and developing personas for decades as a means of focusing on what creative messages to deliver and identifying who is best positioned to buy our products.

The AIDA funnel, a stimulus-response model developed in 1898 (see Figure 2.1),[2] is another marketer tool that has changed

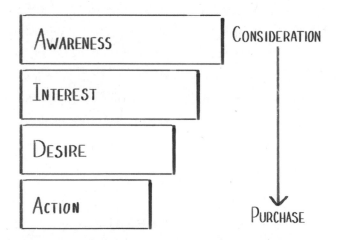

Figure 2.1 **The AIDA funnel was invented in 1898 by E. St. Elmo Lewis, an early advertising pioneer. The concept persists to this day, as a way of defining how consumers move through a sales cycle from consideration of a product to its purchase.**

little since its invention. "Awareness, interest, desire, and action" make up the reigning conceptual framework that marketers use to think about the motion of consumers. In the data-rich environment we live in today, however, neither the segment nor the funnel adequately corresponds to the actual behavior of customers as they zig and zag their way toward an outcome of interest to a modern marketer (see Figure 2.2).

Want to advertise a new pair of sneakers to an audience of millennials and generation Zers? Today, the baseline for that includes a social strategy spanning five major outlets, an online display strat-

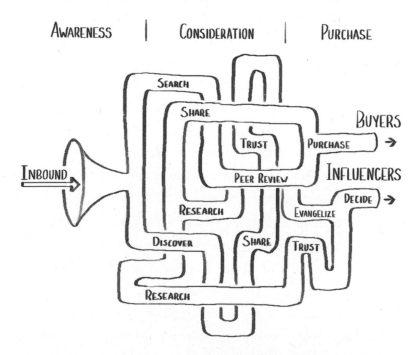

Figure 2.2 **A depiction of the twists, turns, and multiple channels in the modern marketing funnel. Today's customer journey includes factors such as search, social, product comparison sites, and e-commerce experiences—and impacts both buyers of brands and the people who influence buying decisions.**

egy across thousands of websites, video initiatives, separate land-ing pages, a broadcast television and cable television buy, targeted e-mail, in-game sponsorships, print advertising, and an in-store beacon strategy. And that's just the media side of the equation. Once you've found a customer, the post-sale effort to engage him or her in a cross-sell or upsell involves equally complex coordination across CRM, point-of-sale, and multidevice interaction systems.

The fundamental problem isn't the explosion of channels. That's merely a symptom of the fact that millennials, who now constitute a larger cohort of Americans than baby boomers,[3] sim-ply don't consume mass media and engage in steps from aware-ness to action as they did 60 years ago. They don't tune into television as often as other age groups. They spend their time on mobile devices and video consoles, and they spread their atten-tion across hundreds of websites during the limited time they are on desktop computers.[4]

Compounding the problem is the fact that they are fully in control of the brands they engage with. Bad flight? Now, @Delta has to respond to that angry tweet through its social media "war room." Sneakers wearing down too soon? Customers will kill you with Yelp reviews and, worse yet, rant about it to a surprisingly large audience of sneaker fanatics on a specialty blog. They might decide to call your brand something else entirely—and the name can stick, despite millions of dollars in investment. Millions of people call Dove's ubiquitous Beauty Bar of soap by the name "Silk" thanks to the packaging. The company simply goes with it.

The funnel is dead. We now work to engage consumers whose trajectory looks like a snake,[5] a bowl of spaghetti,[6] or any number of nonlinear shapes.[7] Your customers might first find you on social media through a recommendation, engage with several of your online ads, go to a store and check out the product, and visit your website and a product page, before finally purchasing on a partner's e-commerce site. It gets even more complicated when you are dealing with a known customer with whom you are interacting via e-mail, direct mail, and mobile channels.

In a context in which people are connected and constantly on the move, the basic concepts of a segment or a persona start to lose their relevance. They were good-enough approximations of who we were in a predigital context, but they're far too simple when we're awash in systems and data that can capture all our individual nuances and quirks. People are not static beings marching predictably from awareness to interest to desire to action. The successful modern marketer begins with the recognition of the consumer as zigging and zagging, dynamic, and always in flux: less of a human being, more of a *human becoming*.

Think about the typical suburban, upper-middle-class father from a segmentation standpoint. He is always going to be in the dad segment, will not change much from an income standpoint until retirement, and is highly unlikely to move locations with great frequency. If he's a sports lover, he's always going to love sports, and if he has been traveling for work with any frequency, he is likely to remain a business traveler until he retires. Those attributes are static and do not change from month to month or even year to year. When marketers segment their audiences, they almost always describe buyer personas in this way.

But that dad is many different people depending on the weather, his location, the time of day, and what he is doing. He could be a high-income business traveler during the week but turn into an "extreme sports enthusiast" on the weekend. He can be a dad on Saturday morning when he is coaching his son's soccer game and a foodie later that night when he is out in the city with friends. He can be a Powerade intender before Thursday night hoops, and a Diet Coke intender Sunday afternoon during a weekly grocery store run.

CASE IN POINT

Meredith Redefines "Momness"

Meredith Corporation, one of the world's most successful women's publishers, with properties such as Better Homes and Gardens, American Baby, Country Life, and AllRecipes.com, has deeply internalized this new reality. Advertisers interested in reaching the "household CEO" turn to Meredith for its high concentration of influential women, those who ultimately decide what food the family members eat, what sofa they sit on, which cars they drive, what clothes they wear, and where they will bank and invest. But like the dynamic suburban dad, there are many different flavors of the "Meredith mom."

For Alysia Borsa, CMO and chief data officer of Meredith Corporation, data was the key not only to discovering what defined the women coming to various Meredith properties, but also to understanding what determines their loyalty to the brand and, ultimately, their likelihood to engage with Meredith's deep pool of advertisers. By letting go of the idea of one kind of mom, Alysia and her team discovered the thousands of combinations and angles that define a mom on the move, continually in the process of becoming. "Meredith's women are obviously a great advertising demographic, but advertisers are increasingly seeking more defined segments of readers, and they need to engage with our audience in relevant ways in real time," says Borsa. "Not only did we need to understand what defined the 'momness' of a site like American Baby, but we wanted to understand at a very granular level what kinds of food AllRecipes users were interested in at that moment."

Borsa and her team developed a segmentation strategy that enabled them to build audiences on demand for advertisers, supported further by an in-house capability to tune their ads according to the particular recipes that their consumers are viewing. The data-driven advantage of Iowa-based Meredith has propelled the corporation into a power position within the highly competitive publishing sphere. In 2018 it acquired the iconic publisher Time Inc. for $2.8 billion.[8]

Not long ago Internet travelers were tethered to desktop computers. Today, mobile devices keep us constantly connected. They know where we are, what the weather is like, and much of what we are doing. Although we intuitively understand this shift toward always-on connectivity and the possibilities for self-expression and the immediate gratification that it affords, too many companies continue to treat us as if we were frozen in time. They're like the affable but clueless relatives you see during the holidays who insist on interacting with you as if you were a toddler or a grade schooler, refusing to see that you've grown up.

Mindsets precede methods. The first, most vital step on your path to data-driven excellence is to stop looking at all suburban dads and cereal moms the same way and to embrace the human becoming. Companies like Meredith reject the notion that consumers can be put into tidy boxes marked with rigid labels. By organizing their initiatives around the principle that they will never see the same consumer twice, they lay down an enduring foundation for future investments, strategies, and tactics in marketing.

PRINCIPLE #2: YOU HAVE MORE DATA THAN YOU THINK . . . AND YOU THINK YOU HAVE MORE DATA THAN YOU ACTUALLY DO

The good news is that there's more missing but knowable data within reach than you initially surmise. The less good news is that your own data is less valuable and less complete than you might like to believe.

When we first started talking to big marketers, some of the first who came on board were global consumer products companies, brands such as Kellogg's, Mondelez, Heineken, and Anheuser-Busch InBev. Kellogg's had arrived at the party early and had managed to assemble millions of e-mail addresses via "Family Rewards," a subscription program offering coupons and points for shopper loyalty. While impressive, a few million e-mail addresses is small change relative to the billions of people across the world who recognize and buy Kellogg's brands. The company's primary distributors tend to be big-box retailers, companies like Walmart that own the in-store consumer relationship with the consumer. Kellogg's 2016 financial report states it plainly: "During 2016, our top five customers, collectively, including Wal-Mart, accounted for approximately 34 percent of our consolidated net sales and approximately 47 percent of U.S. net sales."[9] In other words, Kellogg's, like many other consumer goods companies, did not own a one-to-one relationship with its customers.

It's a difficult situation to be in, given the way the planet tilts. Customers increasingly expect companies to treat them as Netflix and Amazon do, but without understanding that brands like Kellogg's stand at arm's length from the sale. It would be easy for traditional marketers to assume they don't have a seat at the data-driven table. Persistent, innovative marketers at Kellogg's, however, realized early that they had a great deal more data than they at first thought.

Their leverage from data started with the hundreds of millions of dollars they were investing in digital advertising. Kellogg's realized that cookie and ad delivery data offered a valuable insertion point into the world of consumer data. The company started combing through the data to understand, for example, how many ads were being seen by the same users. Where were the ads appearing, and how many people were seeing them? High ad viewership on cooking sites, for example, gave Kellogg's a sense that consumers were more engaged with their brand while they were preparing a meal. The e-mail addresses in the Family Rewards database, while not as huge as the cookie pools, were extremely valuable because they were tied to known users whom they could reach via e-mail campaigns. Kellogg's could also see those same users whenever they logged in on mobile phones, tablets, and desktops, and the company could tailor its messages accordingly.

The data that Kellogg's was capturing from its own advertising and web properties is *first-party data*. It's a valuable entry point for a conversation with a consumer, and for marketers new to the data game, it's an easily underestimated source of power.

But the power of data doesn't stop with the collection of signals from your own websites, apps, and media campaigns. That's merely the beginning. ConAgra, another consumer goods company that started with a data scarcity mindset, quickly uncovered a wealth of opportunity not just in its own first-party data, but in its partners' data as well. This is *second-party data*, data from a named partner made available through an authorized data-sharing agreement. ConAgra's second-party relationships with partners such as Meredith, for example, enabled it to find more Hunt's Tomatoes customers on AllRecipes.com., one of Meredith's premium media sites.

Not only did these companies own more data than they thought; they also had access to enormous pools of second-party and highly available *third-party data*, which can be purchased from data brokers such as Experian, IRI, Oracle Datalogix, Acxiom, Alliant, and comScore. Third-party data providers essentially do two things: first, they aggregate website behavior, purchase information, and monitor other signals from companies with their own first-party data; second, they group them into segments such as "travel intenders" or "foodies." In this way, third-party data providers are to data what ad networks are to advertising inventory: they aggregate and curate data and thereby provide scale to companies that cannot achieve meaningful data density on their own. There are many dozens of third-party providers peddling hundreds of thousands of segments to any company that wants to buy them, and almost all digital marketers use third-party data of some kind in moderate quantities. We don't know of any companies that use first- or second-party data to the exclusion of third-party data or vice versa. Because third-party data has become so plentiful and inexpensive, however, most marketers and publishers find greater relative value and more competitive differentiation in first-party data.

The flip side of the paradox is when marketers become too sure of the data at their disposal and inattentive to the continual need to expand it over time. Data has no end point; it's a habit that demands commitment to continual cultivation. We have encountered companies a little too cocksure of their data dominance and watched them suffer from the complacency it spawns.

One of our publisher clients amassed an impressive base of highly engaged consumers measured in the many tens of millions. It felt confident in its ability to grow its advertising business based on this reach. When we started to unpack the nature of the data, however, a glaring shortcoming immediately came to light. The company built its offering exclusively as an app; there was no access to its service via a browser on a desktop computer. While this appeared prescient at first blush in the way it recognized consumers' preference for mobile content, it also exposed a significant shortcoming: without the ability to connect users across both mobile and desktop experiences (as Kellogg's did with its Rewards data), it was at a considerable disadvantage when it came to enabling marketers to customize experiences for consumers across both surfaces. While desktop usage as a fraction of total screen time has declined, the reports of its death have been greatly exaggerated. Most marketers are looking for integrated media covering all of the average consumer's relevant touchpoints.

"But we have 120 million unique users!" they proudly reminded us during many of our early meetings. Our client-facing leaders were put in the unpopular position of having to explain that their data wasn't as precious or complete as they had thought. They subsequently undertook a significant product initiative, which required meaningful investment over two years, to close the gap.

Internally, this became an instance of what we refer to as the "Don't get too big for your britches" rule. We developed silky scripts to explain to our more overconfident customers that their data sets weren't as large and as powerful as they thought. We never relished those conversations.

CASE IN POINT

Pandora Uses Second- and Third-Party Data to Learn More About Its Listeners

Pandora enjoys direct connections with consumers via the device on which they spend most of their time: their mobile phone. Unlike our other customer, however, Pandora makes its service available across browsers, apps, and other devices where its users are required to log in. This furnishes Pandora with the ability to recognize customers across multiple devices—mobile, desktop, cars, Amazon Echo, even Samsung refrigerators—and this, in turn, arms it with powerful information about the context in which its listeners are using the service. Someone listening to a workout mix is likely to be exercising. Someone playing "Kids Jamz" is almost 100 percent likely to have a child between the ages of 6 and 12.

Pandora's Music Genome analyzes thousands of individual music attributes to understand the DNA of a song, thereby giving Pandora the ability to recommend new content to users based on whatever they've previously enjoyed. When it gets it right, which is most of the time, people stay engaged on the Pandora app for hours at a time. They even help Pandora by giving a "thumbs up" or "thumbs down" to individual tracks so Pandora can tweak its algorithms to personalize playlists for each of its millions of users.

As much as Pandora knows about people's musical tastes—as well as how, when, and where they listen—it doesn't know who likes Budweiser more than Heineken. It cannot, for example, tell an auto intender from a travel intender. As one of the world's largest media companies, Pandora pays the bills by selling targeted advertising to the world's largest brands. To enrich its advertising products for marketer clients and to claim full value from its considerable base of monthly listeners, Pandora needed to close these gaps. David Smith, Pandora's SVP of monetization and yield, recognized early that going it alone wasn't going to work. He needed technology to incorporate second- and third-party data to extend Pandora's understanding of its consumers (see Figure 2.3).

"Although we got very good at building out proprietary segments from our data—things like age, gender, and location—we knew we needed to stay on the cutting edge of

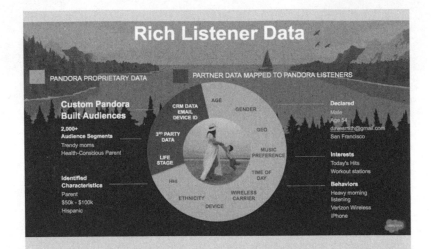

Figure 2.3 **Pandora has a great deal of proprietary information about its listeners, but it turns to shared partner data for enrichment.** (*Source: Pandora*)

data strategy to meet the needs of ever more sophisticated marketers," said Smith. "We are always looking for ways to enrich what we have to meet the needs of marketers looking for very specific segments such as Hispanic audiences, fashion-conscious moms, or travel intenders."

PRINCIPLE #3: THERE IS NO TRUTH, JUST MORE AND LESS USEFUL THEORIES

Successful business executives are lauded for their conviction and decisiveness. We're all encouraged to show up at the big meetings with the big dogs and put a stake in the ground. Curiosity is perceived as tenuousness. Business books like this one are positively reviewed when they present definitive guides.

We think that's all hooey. There is no truth. There is no certainty. In the modern marketing context especially, there are only more and less useful theories, successful marketers who stand ready to revise them, and has-beens clinging to false precision.

If you subscribe to the human becoming, then Principle #3 is, arguably, its necessary consequence. In our dealings with leading marketers, however, we've seen many commit to Principle #1 but then adopt multiyear marketing playbooks that fail to anticipate the flickering in consumer tastes that the marketers already know is coming. It's like a master meteorologist who predicts regular, heavy rainstorms but insists on building a house in a place where it's easily washed away in a mudslide. Principle #3 translates the idea of the human becoming into concrete action. When it comes to operationalizing new hypotheses about consumers, its prescription for the modern marketer is to let a thousand flowers bloom.

Jon Suarez-Davis (JSD), the former head of global media at Kellogg Company, is familiar with the challenges of implementing targeted marketing at scale. An early digital pioneer and self-described data hound, JSD was one of the first CPG (consumer packaged goods) marketers to deploy a data management platform, understanding how consumers were becoming harder to reach with one-to-many vehicles such as broadcast television and print. Like other large consumer products companies, Kellogg's faced a scenario in which changing consumer tastes resulted in people abandoning mass-produced processed foods and glomming onto labels that boasted "organic," "GMO free," and "gluten-free."[10] Big manufacturers move more slowly than consumer tastes. Every change to a new product or line extension may require a plant upgrade, new manufacturing process, and supply chain adjustments that reverberate through the entire organization. Kellogg's marketing team had to quickly adapt to the ever-shifting tastes of its wide range of customers.

The challenge for a marketer like JSD was to start moving working media dollars into the channels where tomorrow's consumers were gathering, maintain momentum for classic brands, create a new segmentation model that could adapt to a broad set of category buyers, and ensure Kellogg's had the right tools in place to measure whether it was spending its marketing dollars in an optimal way. Much of that work involved bringing in the tools for one-to-one marketing and technology partners that could deliver on that promise.

But what if pure one-to-one marketing wasn't the right approach at all? One of our favorite moments during a big CPG pitch was hearing JSD explain how *missing the target* sometimes created new opportunities for growth. Despite the obsession with building marketing capabilities that promise the "right message, place, and time" for every addressable interaction with customers, a big debate today concerns whether or not personalization can perform at scale. After all, what big product marketers crave is reach—the ability to drive brand consideration widely and to drive more lift in the stores where people buy their goods.

"One of the things that always amazed me was how much effectiveness we could get out of the 50 percent of media we measured as being off-target," JSD said, adding, "Sometimes when you miss, you end up hitting the target anyway. We had campaigns where our agency missed our targeted demographic by miles, and found out later that we were getting sales from unexpected age groups. We saw this in a Pringles campaign, where a lot of sales were coming from Baby Boomers—ironically, a demographic we were explicitly not trying to target."

In a world where Facebook offers the ability to target large swathes of the human race at granular levels, and there are literally tens of thousands of prepackaged data segments to use for targeting online, this becomes a powerful, actionable insight. But data-driven targeting has two fundamental flaws that inhibit its effectiveness. First, it is expensive. The more data you add to a media campaign, the more expensive and narrow the targeting becomes. Just targeting snack lovers for Pringles excludes the shopper who is buying Morningstar Farms vegetarian burgers for her flexitarian daughter on the same trip to the grocery store.

Second, segmentation almost always leads to observational bias. Observational bias occurs when the researchers subconsciously build the parameters of an experiment to prove their hypothesis. For marketers, it's the "moms buy minivans" problem. When we design our initial customer segmentation, we start with what we know. But what if there are hidden insights and valuable gems lurking beneath the surface that we can easily miss because we're not looking for them, or worse, are actively seeking to confirm their nonexistence?

Take a high-end running shoe made by Brooks. Most people who buy Brooks sneakers are hard-core runners or marathoners, and there is a cultish devotion to this segment among the Brooks marketing team. But there are also a lot of hipsters out there who love Brooks's throwback style and may never move faster than a brisk walk on their way to a bowling night in Brooklyn or Oakland. The point is simple. If you segment against marathoners, then you're only going to target marathoners, measure your ability to reach them, and miss the hipsters altogether.

**RB and the Campbell Soup Company
Build Intelligent Theories About
Consumer Behavior That Transcend
Segmentation (and Sell More Soup!)**

Innovative marketers tucked back in a value chain like Kellogg's or Warner Bros. knew they needed to be fearless in mounting a new theory of their consumers and relentless in testing and measuring whether or not it worked. The challenge becomes even more acute for a company like the United Kingdom–based RB, formerly known as Reckitt Benckiser. When it goes to market with Mucinex, it's effectively trying to find individuals who have a cold. Who are they? Where do they live? How do we persuade them to engage or buy the product, especially at the moment they're feeling so miserable? It is, possibly, the hardest challenge in theory creation and revision.

Like every other marketer, RB is trying to get a personalized message to increasingly hard-to-find consumers: Mucinex clears your sinuses when they're stuffed up. People rely on Mucinex to get them back to work after an allergy attack, so people with allergies are an attractive segment. The problem is that, unlike other household staples, medicine is not something people think of buying *before* they catch a cold. They consider purchase when they start to feel sick. RB runs branding campaigns throughout the year with its "Snot Monster" mascot[11] to make sure Mucinex is top of mind when that moment of truth hits individual cold and allergy sufferers. On a limited budget, you might not have enough discretionary money when cold and flu season starts.

RB doesn't wait for its customers to come to them. It builds a theory of where and who they are and when they need Mucinex, and it gets to work. Mucinex advertising starts to flow in targeted areas that report a high incidence of flu and cold or high pollen counts that affect allergy sufferers. It leverages past purchase behavior to make sure it is targeting people who are known buyers of over-the-counter medicines with a demonstrated susceptibility to allergies. Combine a high-pollen count with structured geographic targeting, and its attack plan is complete. It continually updates and revises its approach, layering on a display coupon and testing whether it works for the subgroup to which it was targeted.

The Campbell Soup Company's core product (soup) represents another interesting example of the need to build and continually revise an intelligent theory of the consumer. Before we talked to its marketing team led by head of global media Marci Raible, we assumed soup was something shoppers threw into their supermarket carts with regularity. It turns out that a few key drivers determine purchase behavior. Campbell's Soup sells a lot more soup when the weather turns bad and people are stocking the pantry to ride out a storm, expecting to spend several

(continued)

days inside. As with Mucinex, it is a simple but actionable insight, one that can be applied to a personalized digital marketing campaign fueled by weather forecast data. In fact, the Campbell Soup Company is famous for its "misery index," which tracks bad weather across the United States. Upward ticks in the misery index trigger revised messaging and advertising activities across radio and other media in local markets.[12]

"Campbell's has been using data to target advertising for decades," says Raible. "It's all about trying to reach our customers when they are in the right mindset to digest our message. In some cases, that means trying to drive consumption, so we can move cans out of the pantry. In other cases, it's about driving purchase behavior. In still other cases, it's about announcing a new product or getting awareness about the new version of an old favorite. Our challenge is using data to make sure we align the right message with the right customer, and make them feel Campbell's understands them as a person."

What Mucinex and Campbell's Soup have in common is a central theory of the consumer that unifies their marketing tactics, but that can be flexibly updated on the fly.

You don't know what you don't know, and you stick to what you know at your own peril. Building a theory of your consumer requires working from what you know through data-derived assumptions that you make about your buyers, but you must also be flexible enough to anticipate reaching customers you never thought you had. It means embracing mistakes and learning from botched targeting. Successful marketers proceed with a child's mindset: curious about new possibilities, unafraid to make mistakes, ready to explore, free of limits or predetermined ideologies about where to go.

CHAPTER 3

DATA IN, DATA OUT

Famously, Byron Sharp's book *How Brands Grow* challenged the idea that consumers needed or wanted a "relationship" with a brand at all.[1] "When you look at the data," he argued, "what works in branding is surprisingly simple—making the brand easy to buy—by maximizing its physical availability and creating an attractive and memorable set of distinctive brand assets; sensory and semantic cues such as colours, packaging, logo, design, taglines and celebrity endorsements that make the brand easy to like, memorise and recall." In a nutshell, Sharp posited that you need two things to grow a brand: some shelf space in the consumer's mind and some physically available shelf space in a store near the consumer. This approach worked in the days when it was easy to influence the majority of consumers across mass marketing channels like TV and when there were fewer products and more available shelf space. It fails in the era of connected devices, seamless online commerce, social media, and the seemingly uncapped complexity they've spawned.

Ad technology has become a secret club where everyone speaks a strange language full of acronyms and code words. Its jargon (DSPs, SSPs, RTB, "header bidding," etc.) has become a fence raised to keep out the nonspecialists, while permitting those within the fence to continue with the belief that what they do is too hard and too technical to be questioned. The "LUMAscape" created by Terence Kawaja gives form to this cacophony as it maps the thousands of ad technology companies sitting between marketers and publishers. Figure 3.1 is the LUMAscape for display advertising—and there are 18 companion maps of equal complexity for video, mobile, social, and other technology categories. Ironically, this depiction is frequently used in investor pitches when a new company seeking funding trots out the LUMAscape

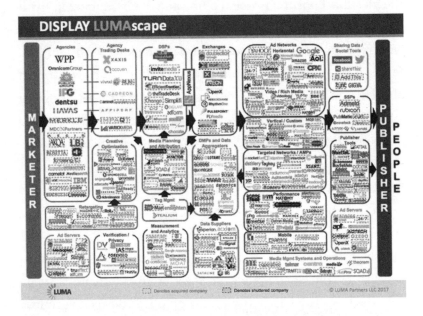

Figure 3.1 **Terence Kawaja created his landscape map when he was a partner at GCA Savvian Partners. It is often featured in investor presentations as proof of the complexity of digital marketing.**
(*Source: LUMA Partners*)

and claims to shrink the distance between marketers and publishers; some months later, it finds itself added to the map and engulfed in the complexity it sought to eradicate.

In the world of display advertising, more than 60 percent of working media dollars find their way into ad technology companies before they make it into the hands of a publisher (see Figure 3.2).[2] A big marketer like Anheuser-Busch InBev, worried about losing market share to craft beer brands, might want to get its message out about the heritage of its Budweiser brand to an impressionable, of-age generation Z consumer on a publisher such as Vice, for example. Depending on the configuration of clever ad tech products that both companies use, $10 in "working" media may only end up netting $2 or $3 for Vice. In the end, Anheuser-Busch InBev expends 80 percent of its media investment on all the ad tech middlemen intermediaries between them and Vice, while Vice receives value that is not proportionate to its premium audience. This is what economists call an "inefficient" equilibrium, because too much overhead is involved in the effort to have supply meet demand.

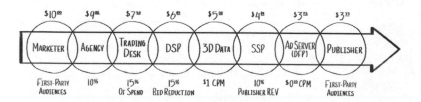

Figure 3.2 **A depiction of the typical flow of media budgets spent programmatically in which, after incurring the "ad tech tax" of vendor fees and data costs, $10 in budget translates to less than $4 of "working" media spend.**

Marketers want precision reach: to find as many people interested in their products as possible and serve them an experience (an ad, an offer, a piece of content) that draws them closer to their brand. Publishers generate content experiences that compel audiences to spend time on their favorite websites, apps, and channels. What underpins most of the LUMAscapes is the challenge, common to both marketers and publishers, of capturing and making sense of people data from so many different sources.

Certainly the most gripping (and possibly most unnerving) thing about technology is that new entrants relentlessly seek to climb to higher ground and quickly subsume or obviate everything that came before. The cacophony of three-letter acronyms captured in the LUMAscape continues as of this writing, as new sub-species such as "customer data platforms" and "data lakes" purport to solve all of the ills of the prior generation's offering. While the differences among them are potentially interesting to vendors, bankers, and market analysts, from our vantage point they all hang together under the banner of data management. Wise operators will steer clear of efforts to push distinctions with vanishingly small differences (CDP versus DMP, for example), and focus instead on understanding and applying what we believe is a simpler, more enduring idea: Data In, Data Out.

CASE IN POINT

Georgia-Pacific Moves from Scarcity to Abundance in the Data Sphere

In early 2015, we were at a CMO conference during which vendors conducted 40-minute meetings with big marketers. We were lucky to spend some time with Douwe Bergsma, the chief marketing officer of Georgia-Pacific's consumer business. Douwe greeted us warmly and then got right down to business. "Kate Metzinger, our media leader, believes we need a data management platform. You may be wondering why a company that sells toilet paper, paper towels, and napkins needs such a technology. We thought perhaps you could answer the question for us."

This seemed like the challenge we were waiting for. While we had helped other CPG brands (notably, Kellogg's, Heineken, and L'Oréal) segment, analyze, and acti-vate audiences for different brands, how could we help Georgia-Pacific better connect with the consumers who buy paper napkins once a month? Georgia-Pacific sells everyday products that people buy often and largely take for granted. As Douwe puts it, "Georgia-Pacific sells toi-let paper, a product consumers don't want to discuss and are typically eager to forget." Sure, the company's Brawny paper towel brand battles for share of market with Procter & Gamble's Bounty brand every single day. Like every other large CPG company, it fights fiercely for every inch of supermarket shelf space. It also battles for mental shelf space. We all develop strong brand preferences over time and have our reasons for being loyal to certain brands and products, thanks largely to advertising.

But why were the CMO and media leader of a paper products company interested in talking to us about data management? Georgia-Pacific's consumers were already in supermarkets and club stores where Georgia-Pacific had

(continued)

strong retail partnerships, plenty of shelf space, and a highly active shopper marketing program. Did brands like Dixie paper cups really need data management to succeed?

Georgia-Pacific knew relatively little about its Dixie cup customers outside of the limited number of people who signed up for coupons or visited the Dixie website. Like every other large consumer products company, Georgia-Pacific utilized surveys and measurement from companies such as IRI and Nielsen. It had a very clear and well-informed view of buyer personas, its share of market, and the competitive landscape. When it came to online data about its customers and potential customers, there wasn't a lot to collect. Kate's team had done some early experimentation with data management, but she and her team were looking to build a solution from the ground up that could help start to connect the magic of Georgia-Pacific's brand advertising with the granular data of the modern consumer.

The company had recently started to deepen digital partnerships, inking a deal with Meredith, as discussed previously, the publisher of well-known women's sites such as Better Homes and Gardens, Parents, and AllRecipes.com.[3] A "Take Back the Table" campaign featuring Vanity Fair napkins created great content for busy moms who wanted to have more family dinners. This initiative gained a lot of traction with moms who were sick of cell phones at the table and overscheduled kids who never seemed to have time to sit down for a family dinner. Moms were going to Twitter and other social outlets with the #TakeBackTheTable message, and Georgia-Pacific supported a Pinterest page featuring tips on setting a table for fast but family-friendly meals. The company was leveraging the creative side of digital and building great content that resonated with the parents who did the shopping for the household.

After our meeting, Douwe stood up and addressed the room. "The opportunity we must seize is to connect the art of our creative approach with the new science of marketing." It was an elegant way of articulating the challenge. Even with its progressive approach to native creative executions, its deep partnerships with leading-edge digital publishers, and its embrace of new social platforms, Georgia-Pacific needed a technology infrastructure to manage people across those channels and to create a capability for handling identity to support its performance measurement efforts.

Unlike Cars.com or Hotels.com, companies that were rich with real, deterministic people data (users who would register with their e-mail, mobile phone number, or address and start a personal relationship with a brand), Georgia-Pacific had relatively few CRM records and, like most CPG companies, was at arm's length from customers who overwhelmingly bought its products at retail. What Georgia-Pacific *did* have was millions of dollars in addressable media spending, from which data signals could be harvested and associated with people. Every click, video view, and social interaction of these anonymous customers could be used to inform a richer customer profile. Georgia-

(continued)

Pacific was, in other words, confronting Principle #2 head on: while the company didn't have as much data as it might have preferred, it was in possession of an abundance of data with which to begin.

Consciously or not, Kate and Douwe had adopted Principles #1 and #3 and inculcated them across their organization. To inject more science into the art of marketing, Douwe and his team would need to do what scientists do: they would need to apply facts, data, and logic to build new theories of their consumers, who were zigging and zagging like subatomic particles in a supercollider. Like good scientists, they would need new equipment to measure the phenomena they were seeking to understand, to quickly launch and conduct new experiments, and to capture the data that resulted. To that end, they resolved to invest in and master new machinery known as data management platforms (DMPs).

DATA IN: EVERY SCRAP OF DATA FROM EVERY POSSIBLE SOURCE

Although data management platforms had been around for a long time, initial use cases for the technology centered on big publishers seeking to better monetize online audiences. Before 2014, only the most sophisticated marketers had adopted DMPs, beginning to make a market for the software. The marketers we met knew enough about DMPs to be curious and understood some of the basic use cases we could help with, but the marketers rarely understood all the ways that the data could transform their enterprise.

The education process usually amounted to our picking up a whiteboard marker and starting to map out what the data marketers actually had—how we would collect it, store it, and make it available to their partners. We called this the "TIE fighter" drawing because, when completed, it looked like the Imperial TIE fighter from *Star Wars*: a "wing" on the left with all the data about every consumer going into our system; a circular middle, representing a unique consumer; and a right wing, evoking all the execution systems to which we would send data to create more valuable experiences for that same consumer. It looked something like Figure 3.3.

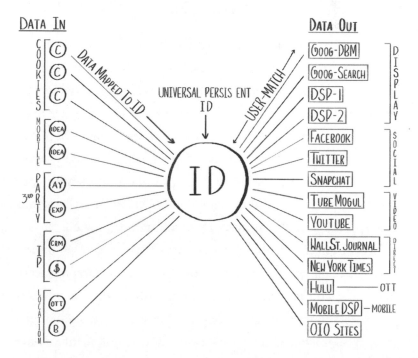

Figure 3.3 **DMPs take in all kinds of disparate data, associate it with a single ID corresponding to every consumer, and send instructions to execution platforms for personalization. The "TIE fighter" picture captures the complexity of a marketer's identity challenge as well as the core functionality of a data management platform.**

The left-side wing included all the different ways that marketers could collect people data and use it to inform their understanding of consumers: online cookies, mobile IDs, beacon signals, second- and third-party IDs from partners, and even anonymized CRM and sales data. Until data management technology came along, marketers understood a single person as a conglomeration of several dozen IDs: cookies from multiple browsers and computers, mobile IDs from phones and tablets, and different partner IDs from various data providers.

Cookie Data

For marketers—especially those with limited CRM data—every signal counts. As we described in Chapter 1, the advent of the Internet opened up exciting new doors for understanding consumer behavior. The ability to track users through cookies[4] started to give marketers new insights regarding the interests and viewing habits of their customers. Marketers who used to rely on survey- and panel-based segmentation started to get a granular understanding of people based on their online behavior and created user personas based primarily on the context of the websites they visited.

As the ability to capture more data on users through online "tags" and event pixels[5] increased, publishers and marketers were able to enrich that contextual understanding with information such as whether or not someone "liked" a site or article, shared a page, or interacted with advertising. Now, true online intent data began to give marketers the ability to score users based on their engagement. Readers who spent more time on a site could add to an understanding of their value; viewers who completed watching an online video had a higher propensity to buy a product and were thus more valuable.

As marketers began to embrace ad-serving technology, they went from depending on their publishing partners for data to collecting their own advertising performance data, which enabled tracking of advertising performance—ad impressions, clicks, and video engagement metrics such as "time spent" with an ad. The Internet promised more accountability, near real-time analytics, and the ability to optimize a campaign in flight based on results. That performance data was initially supplied by the publishers themselves and then through the marketers' own ad-serving reports. Today, as marketers invest in data infrastructure advertising performance data can be matched to an online ID such as a cookie and combined with other data to form a richer picture of campaign performance.

Mobile Data

The smartphone enabled marketers to acquire even richer signals of user intent. Marketers have been touting the "year of mobile" since the 1990s, and for good reason.[6] Mobile phones are nearly miraculous marketing data devices, opening up new insights about people's locations, elevations, movements, weather, interactions with applications, and much more. Big marketers like Procter & Gamble use the term "the moment of truth"[7] to describe how a consumer staring at various choices on a store shelf will select P&G's brand over another, and brands continually study what drives that decision. Why do supermarket shoppers pick Tide washing detergent over Gain?

Today, what sits between the customer and the store shelf is usually a smartphone—a device with access to the Internet, and thereby access to every single review, customer opinion, price, and rating of a product. It's not uncommon to see people scanning grocery products with their phone. And it's very common to see people at Best Buy scanning product reviews of a flat-screen television before they buy it online, a practice known as "showrooming."[8] The idea that brand awareness and product availability were the two primary influencers of the "moment of truth" is still true, but less relevant than ever. Marketers now need to drive brand awareness, maintain high availability in-store and online, deliver near-perfect pricing, and present themselves in the hundreds of places where consumers get information on their brand.

Mobile is certainly the most powerful type of data. The mobile phone not only reveals where a user is, but also what apps he or she interacts with. The advent of mobile payments can connect marketers with real purchase data, to help start "closing the loop" on attribution (did that Facebook campaign actually work?). Marketers who can link online cookies to Apple's advertising ID, or "IDFA,"[9] can also get a sense of how their customers engage across devices, and then they can plan their marketing accordingly.

Third-Party Data

As online pools of cookie identifiers grew into the millions and billions, companies started to segment that data and sell it for user targeting. As outlined in Chapter 2, these off-the-shelf audience data sets are known as third-party data. There are many flavors of third-party data, and most marketers use it to enhance targeting or acquire additional reach. As it's difficult to understand much from a brand-new website visitor, publishers and marketers turn to third-party data to enrich user profiles.

Common data for sale includes age and gender attributes, but the choices are virtually endless. Figure 3.4 shows a small sample of a single data provider. As you can see, Acxiom offers an endless variety of choices: location, behavioral, financial, demographic, lifestyle, and purchase data. There are providers with psychographic data sets that claim to infer personalities and political beliefs, auto data providers that can guess which car you are likely to lease, and even purchase data providers that can tell which type of toilet paper you prefer.

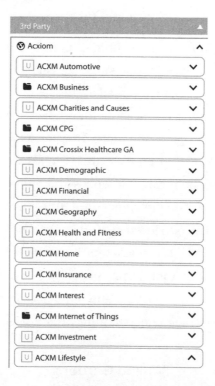

Figure 3.4 **A screenshot of the segmentation menu in a Salesforce DMP. There are dozens of providers and tens of thousands of available audience segments, grouped in various taxonomies.**

Given this availability, marketers began to take their relatively limited website data and combine it with income data from providers like Experian, specialized demographic data from Nielsen to find "suburban pioneers," and location-based data to target designated market areas (DMAs are defined regions where marketers can reach people on television and radio) or even zip codes within a certain distance of a store. For example, visitors to a site like L'Oréal's makeup.com can be matched with third-party data to understand which of them are suburban women with household incomes greater than $50,000.

Social Data

Social data is another rich source of people data. Not only do people identify themselves on sites like Facebook, but they are authenticated through their e-mail addresses and mobile phones. Magically, they also tell us all about themselves—gender, age, race, marital status, education, and more. They tell us what movies they like, what they do for fun, and who their friends are. Most users tell us all about their political preferences and opinions, just as they tell us what their brand preferences are. This is truly amazing people data for marketers to leverage. Today, Facebook and Instagram make that data available to marketers that invest in advertising, and make it accessible only for that purpose. They do not allow marketers to take media exposure data and put it back into their systems so they can enrich their understanding of campaign performance.

Walled Gardens

So-called walled gardens, which refer chiefly to Google and Facebook today, are protected environments where data is self-contained. Like the Hotel California, data can enter but (almost) never leave. It is estimated that Facebook and Google will capture 96 percent of media growth in 2018.[10] In other words, nearly 100 percent of every new media dollar will flow into the hands of these companies, while traditional media companies and smaller publishers fight over the remaining 4 percent. We believe Amazon will enjoy an outsized portion of new media dollars as well, particularly as it ramps up its ecommerce advertising offerings. Why are these platforms so powerful?

It's because of their access to people data. Collectively, Facebook, Google, and Amazon command nearly 10 percent of the market for modern digital experiences. As a result of their gargantuan investments in data management, they capture and make use of all the data that consumers leave behind. Facebook knows everything about us and our friends, Google knows what we are interested in in real time, and Amazon knows exactly what we like to buy and when we want it. Such data is a marketer's dream, but because of its value and due in part to user privacy considerations, these sites rarely let their people data slip outside their walls.

Sometimes, Facebook will share some of its data with a large marketing partner, and the process by which it does so is testament to how seriously it takes user privacy and the value it ascribes to the data it collects. Facebook requires marketers to come to its campus with a laptop that has never been connected to the Internet (a "clean" machine), which might have a customer list loaded on it. Facebook enters the room with a similar clean machine with the data from Facebook campaigns: what ads users saw, etc. The data sets are merged on these two virgin machines, and the advertiser is able to look at aggregate-level data about performance before his or her machine is wiped clean and the advertiser leaves the Facebook campus.[11] Given the recent user privacy pitfalls that Facebook is ensnared in, we wonder how much data the company will choose to share with its advertisers going forward.

CRM and Purchase Data

The building blocks for the most successful customer profiles start with access to customer records, stored inside your CRM database. Marketers' data on customers—name, address, phone number—is perhaps the most powerful asset in their arsenal. In the world of digital marketing where scale is so fiercely coveted, many companies like to boast about the billions of pseudonymous customer profiles (cookies or mobile device IDs) they've collected over time. But as a means of understanding propensity to purchase, a few hundred thousand CRM records trump a million anonymous cookies any day.

When looking for customer intent, there is no truer signal than the data that customers offer you about themselves. It doesn't matter whether your brand is a premium publisher offering a free one-week newspaper trial or a beauty company offering a daily makeup-tips e-mail; customers who "raise their hands" and authenticate online give us permission to know them as real people. Unlike other signals of intent (clicks, page visits, impressions, and the like), customers who declare themselves are high-octane fuel for smarter, more dynamic customer segmentation, the key to turning anonymous consumers into real customers.

For online marketers, the distinction between "deterministic" (i.e., someone has logged in and identified himself on a site like the *Wall Street Journal*) and "probabilistic" signals (using an algorithm to guess that it's the same person on two different devices) is fundamental. As consumers move about and connect on various devices, the key to continuing a marketing conversation relies entirely on the ability to map devices to people, quickly determine their identity, and deliver a relevant message.

One of the principal means of generating deterministic online user data with e-mail addresses is called "onboarding." Onboarding works by taking an e-mail address or other personally identifiable data key (for example, a postal address or telephone number), anonymizing it via a process called "hashing," which turns data into a string of letters and numbers, and matching it to a cookie or another addressable ID. Typically, marketers with a lot of e-mail addresses partner with companies like LiveRamp/Acxiom and Neustar to help them turn those e-mails into cookies.

CASE IN POINT

Dunkin' Brands Leverages CRM Data as a Force Multiplier for Customer Engagement

Although it sounds simple, the idea of matching known data sets (like e-mail) with unknown, anonymous user data (like cookies) is just a first step into the broader challenge, briefly sketched in Chapter 1, of managing the multiple versions of you. When we first met with Dunkin' Donuts, it was grappling with this challenge as part of a long-term project to supercharge its approach to personalized marketing. Just like Keurig Green Mountain, Dunkin' was in a fierce battle

(continued)

for the hearts, minds, and wallets of the American coffee drinker. Its competition ranged from premium coffee chains such as Starbucks to quick-service restaurants such as McDonald's, which was stepping up its coffee game.

Dunkin' coffee shops were places that people could depend on for a highly consistent, fast breakfast or afternoon coffee break. That customer archetype still rings true today: there are "Starbucks people" and "Dunkin' people," and not many in between. Although much of this sentiment is based on regional distribution of the chains,[12] there is no doubt that there are core differences in brand adopters.[13]

Dunkin' was confronting the paradox of Principle #2: the company had a ton of consumer data, but not as much as it needed to get the job done. With rich access to stores of mobile and e-mail data, how could Dunkin' move from a CRM-first data strategy and amplify what it knew about consumers to deliver consistent, fast experiences at massive scale? Was it possible to use its CRM data as a force multiplier to support a broader expansion strategy for customer engagement?

Since 2006, Dunkin's digital team has been re-architecting brand experiences to keep up with fast-moving consumer trends, and a large part of the initiative centered on creating great customer experience. Dunkin' launched an effort to build a first-party relationship with its customers, including the introduction of a new loyalty program, DD Perks. When we met the Dunkin' team, DD Perks had millions of active users, and the company was garnering results from its mobile loyalty strategy.

Customers who ordered via the mobile app could avoid the lines by paying directly through their phones. They could earn free coffee frequently and get special discounts on menu items. Dunkin' connected the app with its in-store point-of-sale systems and tied mobile app usage and in-store sales together. It combined these data sets to get a better understanding of attribution and to build deep profiles of its customers. Now, Dunkin' could present customized menus to its customers based on their frequent choices, and the company could better understand the differences and buying habits between coffee and tea drinkers and test messages for new menu items.

This CRM and purchase data asset formed the foundation for Dunkin's segmentation strategy for anonymous web users: real customer data was telling the company the difference between frozen Coolatta drinkers and classic coffee fans, between early-morning grab-and-go commuters and late-morning in-store coffee drinkers. Connecting these real-life customer profiles with the anonymous world of the Internet would help Dunkin' grow and scale beyond its 5 million known app users, enabling it to intelligently reach tens of millions of new customers.

Location Data

People never leave home without their phone, and phones know where you are, where you have been, where you are going, and how long you stay in one place. For brands trying to build the perfect customer journey, finding out where your customers are at any one time is a prerequisite for offering them the right message.

A big part of this challenge for all marketers is not just having access to such data, but using it in a way that respects their customers' privacy and offers them the ability to choose how to personalize their experience. This is at the heart of Carpenter v. United States, a case currently before the Supreme Court that raises the question of whether tracking people via their mobile phones violates the Fourth Amendment of the Constitution.[14] It's a fascinating debate, as many mobile phone users are unaware of the ability of mobile phone applications to gather location data from users. As with Facebook privacy settings, many users choose not to restrict them through location settings on their handheld devices.

As a significant consequence of the way smartphones work, we now have a global tracking system that can pinpoint mobile phone users to within a few feet of their location. The most precise method uses global positioning system (GPS) software, which gives the phone an ability to communicate with as many as 30 orbiting GPS satellites in space. As evidenced by the turn-by-turn driving directions we receive while we're driving, the data from several satellites can be combined to pinpoint and track a user fairly accurately. Less sophisticated but adequate for advertising purposes is location tracking via cell tower. A single tower identifies the user within the radius of the tower itself; adding two more towers offers the ability to "triangulate" users down to several hundred feet or less.

This data is highly valuable to marketers seeking to offer someone a mobile coupon while in range of a store, just as it would be valuable to marketers trying to prove that their "Come on in and save!" campaign drove people within the radius of a retail location. But what about one's location within the actual store?

Over the past few years, new hardware and software have enabled companies to collect even more granular location data with what are called "beacons." Beacons are tiny hardware devices whose fundamental function is to look for mobile devices within their proximity. When those devices come close enough to a beacon, the beacon gathers the mobile phone ID and lets its owner know that the phone was identified. Many stores have started to install beacons to communicate with users who are on their premises, directing them to sale items. About half of all basketball arenas in the United States use beacon technology to get a sense of how many trips to the beer and hot dog vendor people make during a game. Imagine the use case for a big food marketer like Mondelez trying to activate sales of Velveeta cheese at 7-11.

CASE IN POINT

Freckle IoT Helps Football Fans Find the Velveeta Before the Big Game

This concept came to life when we started working with Neil Sweeney, the head of Freckle IoT, a provider of beacon hardware and software. While running Juice Mobile, a mobile advertising company in Canada, Neil saw how dominant the mobile marketing channel was; it had the ability to

(continued)

connect advertisers with on-the-go customers at scale, and it had the power of location data for marketing. Like it or not, every mobile phone has the ability to track our movements and, with "location services" enabled, every mobile phone can communicate with a beacon to identify our precise location.

One of Neil's projects involved helping CPG marketers get closer to their customers by understanding their store shopping habits with location data. Like other marketers we have discussed, Mondelez, owner of Velveeta and many other prominent CPG brands, was at arm's length from consumers purchasing its products in stores—and the data they leave behind. Velveeta cheese is great for making nachos for a Sunday afternoon football game and highly available in convenience stores like 7-11, where football fans go to pick up beer and snacks before the big game. Beer and chips go together, but what if Mondelez could get these in-market shoppers to take their game-time snacks to the next level with nachos? Location data from mobile phones could tell Mondelez how far its customers were willing to travel to shop for their snacks and what other stores they were shopping in. Mondelez could measure the success of its mobile campaigns and tie successful in-store purchases to all the other messages that customers were exposed to.

Location data was the key to cracking the puzzle. Freckle started with an in-store beacon deployment, which gave Freckle the ability to know exactly where shoppers were in the store. The company also used a technique called "geofencing," which uses latitudinal and longitudinal data from satellites and cell phone towers to measure people in prescribed locations. Freckle drew virtual circles around competitive convenience stores within 10 miles of the targeted 7-11 location to capture users who were shopping at Walmart or another local convenience store.

The plan was to sense users once they came within proximity to the store, use SMS messaging to deliver a coupon offer to the their phone ("Make nachos for the big game"), follow them into the store to a large endcap display with the cheese promotion and product, ask them to present a mobile coupon for a discount, connect with the store's point-of-sale system to see if they actually bought the Velveeta, and then look at what else they purchased (the hope was, the nacho chips and salsa). If you deconstruct that last sentence, you start to realize how ambitious the plan was:

1. Mondelez was pursuing real-time, in-the-moment marketing. Could it make an offer to a customer who was literally walking into a store that sold its product?

2. It was linking an in-store physical display (classic shopper marketing) with digital marketing, two disciplines that rarely intersect and whose practitioners almost never talk to each other.

(continued)

3. It was trying to measure real-life visits to other stores to get a sense of shopping habits and mapping that data against real people data insights, not just survey data.

4. It was measuring the effectiveness of its SMS campaign by seeing whether or not a coupon it delivered mere minutes ago was redeemed.

5. It was going to analyze shoppers' baskets and see what other products cheese buyers were purchasing, data that could be invaluable for co-promotions.

6. It was measuring the effectiveness of an offline promotion by seeing how many consumers stopped in front of the in-store display and tying that data to the people who bought the product—the holy grail of closed-loop marketing attribution.

7. The final piece of the puzzle was to match those in-store, mobile, and purchase activities against all the other digital campaigns and media exposure that those customers had seen previously. Did they see a few display ads or visit the Velveeta nacho recipe site?

Many of these steps had never been executed successfully in isolation; putting them all together into a cohesive campaign was a marketing moonshot. "The problem marketers are trying to solve today is the same one they've been working on for years," says Neil Sweeney. "How many ad dollars did it take me to produce an actionable outcome? Today, the purchase data available to marketers comes highly modeled—and way too late to impact ongoing campaigns. But now we have the data, using beacons, that can tell us if a consumer walked into a store, and we can marry that with ad exposure data and see how our marketing dollars moved the needle. It's a more precise and actionable way to close the loop on attribution."

DATA OUT: CONNECTING PEOPLE DATA TO EVERY CHANNEL

As we observed in Chapter 2, there are multiple versions of you. The "data-in" objective is to map all the surfaces and places where a marketer might see you to the "uber-you" at the center of the *Star Wars* TIE fighter (see Figure 3.3). Marketers who see the 50 different device IDs and online browser signatures corresponding to you face an analogous challenge engaging with you across 50 different channels—the core of the "data-out" challenge.

Data management systems assign a user ID to every person they see. Joe Smith, for example, would be assigned a Krux ID and be known as User123. (The actual identifier is a long string of gobbledygook like the cookie identifiers we saw in Chapter 1, but we'll call Joe "K123" for simplicity.) K123 is a high-income, middle-aged guy who lives in Connecticut, works in finance, owns his own suburban home, has a wife and two kids, has a high credit card limit and a decent credit score, travels a great deal for work and pleasure, and reads lots of content about offshore fishing.

K123 is the kind of profile that most marketers would pay a lot of money to reach, especially those looking to sell Joe his next credit card, boat, or set of patio furniture. The problem is that while the anonymous Internet Joe is known to us as K123, he might be "G234" to Google, "T345" to Twitter, and "F456" to Facebook. Mapping all the inbound identity mappings along the left side of the TIE fighter is important, but the other half of the equation is to manage all the outbound identities along the right side as well. For technical book-keeping reasons, inbound and outbound identities will sometimes, but not always, correspond to each other. Without the outbound identity mappings in order, it is impossible to control the number of messages Joe gets every month, figure out the right sequence of those messages, or understand which channels contributed to the sale of that $15,000 patio set. For this reason, cracking the data-out problem is the precondition for solving message delivery, sequenc-ing, attribution problems, or *any* engagement strategy that depends on controlling and counting consumer touchpoints.

Data out is all about the ability to intelligently provision data about people to the systems and surfaces they visit. In the early stages, this can be as simple as pushing audience segments to Google and Facebook and targeting users with advertising, or it can be as complicated as connecting data to multiple systems to personalize a consumer's trajectory all the way from the first expo-sure to the final purchase of a product online. Just as data in will leverage disparate sources of identity to refine segmentation and optimize our understanding of people, data out is about maximiz-ing the use of people data to optimize the way we communicate and connect with today's dynamic consumers. We will illustrate the idea of *data activation* through three use cases: global delivery management, prospective look-alikes, and data lake exports.

As we've seen, marketers like Dunkin' Donuts and Warner Bros. use an array of touchpoints (display ads, mobile ads, video ads, messaging channels like e-mail and mobile push) to build brand awareness and convert anonymous consumers into known customers. More often than not, each channel and each platform carries out its own bookkeeping to track the quantity and frequency of engagement with K123 (for example, the number of ad views or impressions). Since the interactions are all delivered to the same person, the marketer needs to control the number of messages received over a certain period of time to prevent ad fatigue for the consumer. Furthermore, after the consumer "converts" (i.e., performs the necessary action, such as a product purchase, that the marketer was trying to achieve), then the consumer does not need to be exposed to any more ads or messages for the same product. This ability to control frequency of messages across multiple systems of engagement is called global delivery management (GDM). We'll say more about its practical effects in Chapter 4; for now our aim is to establish the idea.

Marketers frequently seek to build what are called "prospective look-alikes." As the name suggests, the goal is to start with a seed list of users who have purchased a product and build a larger audience of users who are, based on the behavior of the seed users, likely to buy the same product(s). Once the prospective look-alike audience is constructed, the marketer is ready to activate this look-alike audience in any outbound channel or system.

Increasingly, marketers are beginning to build data science and analytics teams to perform proprietary analyses and build in-house machine learning models for attribution, measurement, and propensity. Data lake exports allow the marketer to map these exports back to their internal systems of record (CRM systems, for example). In this way, they represent an interesting pathway for outbound activation, one that depends not on the control or counting of messages, but on the creation of new, proprietary insights.

User Matching

At the center of any activation capability is a gigantic user match table ("match table") with millions of rows and hundreds or possibly even thousands of columns. The rows correspond to individual users; the columns correspond to different systems and sources visited by users. Activation is, in essence, the lightning-fast lookup of entries in the table.

The match table serves as a real-time, continually updated, always-on dictionary for translating K123 to G234, T345, F456— or *any other* entity on the right side of the TIE fighter (see Figure 3.3). These are the multiple versions of you, corresponding to the proprietary keys that every external system uses to identify you. When asked to send an activation instruction to an external system, data management systems use a match table to look up the partner user ID that corresponds to a unique consumer, and then they activate the data in the desired system of engagement using the partner user ID. Notice that, by construction, every system keeps its own set of books. There is no central clearinghouse for precious identity data, just an array of data dictionaries hosted by different DMPs.

Prospecting look-alikes and data lake exports are activated in the respective systems using a batch data transfer mechanism such as Google Cloud Storage or Amazon Web Services S3 (Simple Storage Service). These data sets can be hundreds of gigabytes or terabytes in size, depending on the number of segments being activated and the granularity of data being exported. Accordingly, a batch data transfer—one that's scheduled in advance and exe-cuted not in pieces but as a whole—is the best mode of transport for transferring large volumes of data from one system to another over the Internet.

Unlike prospecting look-alikes and data lake exports, which involve the transfer of large data sets from the DMP into outbound systems, GDM leverages the same user match table maintained by the DMP, but here the data is transferred to the outbound sys-tem in near real time. (It's not necessarily updated by the receiv-ing system in real time, something we'll address further in the next chapter.) In addition to requiring real-time data processing infra-structure, this also requires the DMP to store the user match table and various impression counts in what is called a real-time key-value data store.

Once an organization has collected its highly valuable people data in a single system of engagement, the challenge is to put it to work. Data out is the central means to that end, a critical gear in the engine room of modern marketing. Without it, data management devolves too quickly into generating results that satisfy curiosity but that never translate into tangible value. Once the foundational pillars of data in and data out are in place, a company is ready to exploit the five sources of power for data-driven marketing.

CHAPTER 4

THE FIVE SOURCES OF DATA-DRIVEN POWER

A recent study estimated that nearly half of Fortune 500 companies are already licensing a DMP to manage their customer data, and another half plan on implementing one.[1] For their adopters, the surge of these new technologies portends new moves and new practices. We've been fortunate to observe many of the world's most pioneering companies use new data-driven technologies to achieve things their designers never anticipated or even imagined. From our field studies we've identified five general use patterns that generate the highest returns and reliably recur across sectors and verticals. We call them the *five sources of power* for data-driven marketing (see Figure 4.1). They are:

- **Segmentation ("right person").** Better data about people offers the ability to segment them precisely and increase precision in reaching them.

- **Activation ("right place").** The ability to match data with partners and connect to every system gives marketers the ability to interact with consumers across every addressable touchpoint.

- **Personalization ("right message").** Tailoring the delivery of content on a website (site-side optimization), a search ad, or a display ad (dynamic creative optimization) enables marketers to target individual segments of users in an impactful way that increases performance.

- **Optimization ("right time").** Giving each consumer the optimal number and frequency of messages allows a marketer to achieve new levels of spend efficiency.

- **Insights ("right idea").** A better understanding of what your customers want, when they want it, and how it fuels the virtuous circle continually forward.

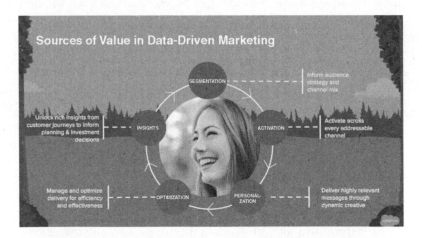

Figure 4.1 **The sources of value for modern marketing consider all the ways a data strategy can be used to impact stages of cross-channel marketing; they describe a self-renewing cycle, where insights drive continuous optimization.**

This cycle of value, from segmentation to insights (analytics), is what progressive marketers have been pursuing since the first banner ads ran 20 years ago. Today we see marketers successfully executing on this vision. In this chapter, we look at how some of the world's smartest data-driven brands are leveraging this framework to drive customer success.

SEGMENTATION: USING PEOPLE DATA TO HIT THE BULL'S-EYE

A few years ago, we were working with an innovative team from Heineken's U.S. marketing group. Its global head of media, Ron Amram, was trying to usher the company into the digital world. Heineken was making big bets on online video and figuring out the technologies it could use to help transform the 153-year-old beer company. It sought to engage with younger consumers, who were increasingly turning to craft beer and away from bigger upscale brands like Heineken and Dos Equis.[2] Heineken wanted to harmonize systems that included data software, media buying, marketing orchestration, and analytics tools to assemble a set of technologies that could help it directly engage with its customers.[3]

It was beginning to shift its marketing budgets away from traditional channels and put more effort into online video, having just forged a relationship with Adobe's TubeMogul,[4] an innovative online video platform that could extend the reach of Heineken's great creative to audiences that watched less broadcast television and more online video. To enhance its strategy, it was testing several data management platforms and deploying deeper analytics for better segmentation across its customer base. We started a proof-of-concept project that focused initially on collecting data from multiple sites and media campaigns.

When we think of segmentation, we usually anchor on attributes like site visitation (Who has actually been to Heineken.com?), past purchase behavior (Who already drinks Heineken?), and contextual signals (What content do these potential Heineken buyers like to consume?). Most consumer goods companies create dozens of personas around their brands: "fun lovers" who drink lots of light beer, "craft lovers" who drink little but expect a gourmet experience with every bottle, etc.

Amram came to us with an informed view of Heineken's world, thanks to a study the company undertook of consumer beer drinking habits, which helped Heineken understand what brands people liked and where their tastes gravitated. Heineken had three distinct personas for whom it needed to define a targeted engagement strategy:

- **Mainstream.** These were people who were at risk of switching from Heineken brands to mainstream, mass brands like Budweiser and Miller. Maybe they purchased Heineken when they were having friends over for a get-together, but they were likely to make their everyday beer something other than a Heineken brand.

- **Craft.** These were hipsters and gourmands who loved microbrews and wanted to try a new craft beer all the time—people who loved the experience of tasting beer and were attracted to the new beer culture and its different hoppy IPAs, rich stouts, and interesting seasonal beers.

They might see Heineken brands as mass-produced and be at risk to remove them from their repertoire altogether.

- **Loyalists.** These were a core group of Heineken loyalists who had strong brand association with one or more labels. These people were frequent European travelers who associated Heineken brands with overseas visits; international soccer fans who associated Heineken with watching football matches; and also some Latin Americans and African Americans, who were brand loyalists. Heineken needed to speak to the folks in this segment and keep them energized with relevant messaging that reinforced their preference and gave them permission to engage more deeply with the brand.

While a somewhat oversimplified view of its segmentation study (its data was packed with amazing insights about competitive brands, including customer consumption of spirits, ethnicity, income levels, etc.), it was a great framework from which to begin. We helped Heineken take this core framework and enrich it with all kinds of website data, third-party behavioral data, and media data so it could start to target and analyze hundreds of additional, more granular, segments.

Yet even after being enriched, it was still a very static view of the Heineken consumer. Remember Principle #1: embracing the human becoming means that loyal beer drinkers resist such easy categorization. The soccer-loving Heineken Light drinker in the afternoon could easily be at a nightclub drinking Dos Equis the next day. What you imbibe at the Super Bowl with friends is one thing; your preference in hops at an upscale pub could well be another.

Months later, we were at a dinner with Heineken's U.S. chief executive, Ronald den Elzen, and its then U.S. chief marketing officer, Nuno Teles, who were on a Silicon Valley tour to meet with technology partners. Ronald pulled out a neatly folded single sheet of paper from the inside of his suit jacket and carefully unfolded it. "Here is a report I share with my board," he said, showing us a neat spreadsheet. "This is an on-premise sales report, which shows our share in bars and restaurants, by region. This is a type of report card I can show, and we can use it to quickly assess how well we are doing against our competitors in this key channel." It was a powerful insight. This was one of many KPIs (key performance indicators) that kept Ronald and his team up at night, and it offered a weekly report card on one aspect of the business. Every beer drinker in a restaurant has a choice, and sales of Heineken brands against their competitors in popular venues was a healthy way to measure the effectiveness of its marketing.

To clinch the point, the next day Ronald went to the whiteboard to illustrate the way Heineken thinks about the U.S. addressable market (see Figure 4.2). Ronald drew a big circle on the whiteboard, saying, "This is how we see the market opportunity in the United States. There are about 320 million people in the U.S." Then he drew another circle inside. "There are something like 140 million people who are adults—or 'legal drinking age–compliant' as we call them—people who can buy our beer." He drew another circle inside. "Here, we know there are approximately 90 million people who drink some kind of alcohol. It could be beer, wine, or spirits, or all three."

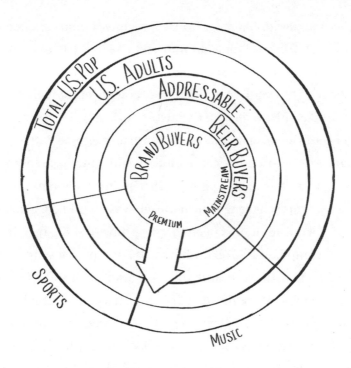

Figure 4.2 **Heineken's simple, yet elegant, vision for understanding their total addressable market.**

As Ronald narrowed into his bull's-eye representation of the Heineken total addressable market, he grew more animated. "Here, in the next ring, we see the category drinkers of beer— about 60 million people who buy and drink beer with enough frequency to make them category buyers." He then completed the bull's-eye. "In the very center are Heineken drinkers, anywhere from 18 to 20 million people in the U.S. who buy and love our brands.[5] Can you help me find these people, and others who are just like them?"

The first challenge for Heineken, Ronald explained, was to grow from the inner circle into the middle circle of beer-category buyers and start to take share from competitive brands. If someone was a beer drinker, Heineken wanted to be in the conversation. Heineken wanted to understand more about that second ring in the circle. Who drank what? Were they craft lovers or mainstream beer drinkers? How receptive were they to a brand message from Heineken? Heineken wanted to put forth an aggressive strategy to reach each camp, and to start winning higher purchase consideration both in store and on premise, in bars and restaurants.

The second challenge for Heineken was around creative execution. Of the additional beer-category buyers and larger group of LDA-compliant drinkers, what message should it send them? Heineken is a global brand and in market with lots of different campaigns. Were these people international football fans? (Heineken was in market with a global International Champions Cup, MLS,[6] and FIFA sponsorships.[7]) Were they into electronic dance music? Heineken supported a global EDM concert series to get in front of millennials.[8] How about general market customers? Were they receptive to Neil Patrick Harris, Heineken's broadcast spokesperson?[9]

Ron wanted the data sliced by creative execution, to understand his market opportunity against people who might be interested in different campaigns. Specifically:

1. How many people were there in the United States who drank beer?

2. What other brands did they drink besides Heineken?

3. How could Heineken reach them?

4. How could Heineken spend less money reaching people who already love their brands?

Here, Heineken was putting Principle #3 into practice. There was no way to get the exact number of potential Heineken customers and loyalists. Heineken's market share was by no means stable either—weather and consumer tastes flicker from day to day. These were modest complications, certainly not enough to deter Heineken from its central objective: to develop the best possible theory, based on the data available, with which to anchor its assessment of its total market opportunity.

For the first question, survey data can provide a reliable answer to how many households in the country drink beer every month. This established the initial bar for the total addressable market report. It seemed like there were approximately 40 million more potential beer consumers in the market, and as many as 30 million more who drank some kind of alcohol who could be open to making beer a more regular choice.

The second question was harder to answer for Heineken, as it does not sell beer directly to customers but rather to supermarkets, wholesalers, and distributors. Companies like Datalogix, IRI, and Nielsen Catalina Solutions buy the data from supermarkets or use surveys to understand brand preference and real-life purchase behavior; then they aggregate the data and sell it to big brands like Heineken. Heineken's main buyers, like those of every other consumer goods company, were retailers, and Heineken did not have a strong enough data connection to its end users.

Knowing we needed real consumer purchase data to deliver our report, we connected with IRI to get a deep look at which consumers who were exposed to Heineken ads drank which beer brands.[10] This enabled us to put together each customer's "repertoire" of brands, mapped to the initial purchase study.

Heineken Light drinkers would occasionally drink other light beer brands. Heineken drinkers stuck to upscale mass brands like Samuel Adams and Stella Artois. Some consumers only drank mass brands like Bud Light or Miller Lite, but would buy Heineken brands when they were entertaining and considered them "party beers."

Finally, we needed to reconcile these people against their preferences, while recognizing that the same user could easily migrate from one segment to another, consistent with Principle #1. Which users across different brand portfolios liked soccer or music or should get the more generic Neil Patrick Harris (or another) creative execution? We needed to dig into consumer behavior from different sets of second- and third-party data and come up with what Heineken's potential reach might be and then slice it by media partner. Once we had these figures, we could build a total market opportunity graph and get a sense of what success would look like for Heineken's digital media campaigns.

This approach has created a sustainable framework for any brand seeking to understand how to approach effective segmentation with data. Like all great advances, it was founded on a very simple concept: tell me how many people I can reach, what other brands I am competing with, and what I can do to get people engaged. The biggest challenge was synthesizing the data, integrating it into Heineken's suite of marketing systems, and building the connections to those customers in the addressable world.

Hershey's Magic Kiss

When Milton Hershey founded his company in 1894, he would have found it hard to imagine the complexities that the Hershey Company would face in the consumer-driven environment of 2018. With a sprawling business portfolio that includes dozens of the world's most popular chocolate and candy brands, a world-famous amusement park, and retail outlets, Hershey Company connects with millions of consumers every day. Even though Hershey Company had a gigantic base of customers who loved the brand, it was not immune to changes in consumer behavior, was reliant on retailers for sales, and was dependent on mass advertising to reach increasingly hard-to-find consumers.

"When I joined Hershey in 2012, we were playing primarily in a category with high penetration, with a wide portfolio of well-known brands," says Charlie Chappell, head of media and integrated communications at Hershey. "We were able to reach 'everyone with a mouth,' using traditional mass reach vehicles very efficiently and effectively. There was no need to put in the time, money, and effort to target precisely. We saw other consumer product companies who had 'overcorrected' and gone too into precision marketing, to the detriment of their business."

(continued)

Mass reach channels like television and print were still effective for Hershey, but over time were showing diminishing returns, as consumers shifted their time and attention to diverse online channels. "Around 2014," Chappell says, "we started to see changing consumer media habits at enough scale to impact the ability of traditional media to reach all of our consumers. We started to expand and learn what digital channels worked and which ones didn't. We experimented with more precise targeting, but were finding many challenges, including selecting the right datasets to use to build our segments. It became clear to us that to compete for the long haul, we had to cultivate our own data."

But how to get there? The challenge for Hershey Company harks back to the struggle faced by Warner Bros., Kellogg's, and many other modern marketers. Millions of people were buying Hershey's Kisses at retail outlets, without providing e-mails or other identification points that Hershey Company could use. In fact, the retailers had more data on Hershey Company's customers than it did. "Just like every other company in our space, we had limited first-party data and couldn't link media exposure to sales, since we don't control the retail channel," says Chappell. "But we couldn't let this stop us from trying to solve the issue."

The team turned to its consumer insights group, led by Ashlee Carlisle, and started to work with its media partners in a "hands on keyboard" approach to understanding what types of third-party data were being used to target potential chocolate lovers by getting into the data management platform and doing segmentation and analytics. It became apparent that it wasn't enough to depend on off-the-shelf targeting data. Hershey Company needed to mine more data from within the company and start getting its hands on valuable purchase data.

"Breaking down silos within Hershey Company was an urgent priority, so that we could cross-pollinate the data we were building and our collective know-how," Chappell says. His team started to pull together all the data it had internally. "We found that we had a lot more than we originally thought. We customized and built an internal analytics tool to produce a brand profile for targeting capabilities. Within the tool we analyzed purchase behaviors, competitive overlap analysis, mind and context, behavioral and psychographic data." This enabled the creation of a new retention and acquisition strategy, aimed both at households who love Hershey Company brands and households who favored competitive offerings—much as Heineken had done.

This intense and relentless focus on first-party data revealed gaps, such as overreliance on age and demographic targeting, but also huge opportunities. Working with Vincent Rinaldi, head of addressable media and technology, Hershey Company started to mine the valuable data sets it had not previously used in media practice. For

(continued)

example, the company conducted a survey, which revealed that people who said Hershey's Kisses was their favorite wrapped chocolate were three times as likely to visit Hershey Park.

"With an amusement park, hotels, and restaurants, our sister organization Hershey Entertainment and Resorts sits on a treasure chest of data," says Rinaldi. "We're working on a data-sharing agreement between the two companies to build out first-party, deterministic profiling for future media buying purposes. The foundation of data storage and collection is being developed, building toward a true one-to-one consumer-facing strategy. An audience-driven strategy will begin with the core consumer. The rest falls into place."

With a new first-party data strategy, Hershey Company has internalized the power of Principle #2 and put it firmly into practice. By humbly beginning from the understanding that it didn't have as much data as it preferred—while also realizing that an abundance of data was readily within reach—Hershey Company rapidly assembled the assets required to fuel a more dynamic approach to segmentation. At least as important, early on it reinforced the practice of extending its data through second-party partnerships to enable a more intimate understanding of its retail customers.

ACTIVATION: FINDING PEOPLE ACROSS
EVERY ADDRESSABLE CHANNEL

Once marketers develop the right segmentation to build a more granular, more dynamic view of their customers, they need to find them and serve up a perfect brand experience. This is extremely difficult for several reasons.

First, the number of addressable channels that consumers use has exploded, as we all give smaller and smaller slivers of our time across mobile, social, desktop, and television channels. Even if you know exactly *who* your consumers are, you need to find them in near real time. Second, if you manage to track them down, you need to target the specific device they happen to be on at the moment. Desktop computer display ads can look tiny and terrible on mobile devices, and even mobile-specific ad executions can suffer if they are not built for a particular operating system or phone. Third, you must have a direct connection to the media partner delivering the ad. If the person is in the market for a case of beer because he's hosting a Friday night party and we can find him reading about basketball on NBA.com, then Heineken must be able to connect its data to that site seamlessly. That's a lot of technical work just to entice someone to buy a few beers.

Back in the day it was enough to create a fun Spuds MacKenzie the Party Animal[11] or Talking Frogs ad[12] to create awareness for Bud Light. Today, we need to create channel-specific brand memes and stories and carefully place them where we suspect individual brand adopters spend time. But how do you discover people with a high propensity for buying your brands in a world fractured into thousands of addressable channels?

For the first several years of our existence at Krux, we were busy helping large media companies organize their audiences so they could make more money selling digital advertising. The notion of "audience management" was not new—online advertising networks had been segmenting people into categories for years—but publishers were just starting to own data management technology and take it in-house rather than relying on third parties. This made total sense, inasmuch as a media company's primary revenue comes from advertising. More granular segmentation leads to more differentiated products; more differentiated products result in higher revenue.

In 2010 we met with a big global news publisher. The publisher was looking for a way to segment users in real time as they came to the news site, and it was trying to decide how much to charge marketers when the users visited. Unknown visitors coming to the site might fetch $1.50 for every thousand ad impressions. But what if the publisher could figure out who those anonymous site visitors were in *real time*, so that a person viewing business content on the site, using a Blackberry (remember, this was 2010) at 6:30 a.m. in New York, could be quickly classified as a "business user"? Those people would be worth as much as $10 per thousand ad impressions—a nearly sevenfold increase. For the publisher, the cost of licensing such a technology would quickly pay for itself.

Data-driven online segmentation proved to be a popular tactic for revenue generation and remains the basis of revenue strategy for major online companies to this day. As we discussed earlier, publishers quickly began embracing data management technology to understand their viewers and sell access to them for higher rates. We were knee-deep in this business, helping all kinds of big media companies implement this strategy, with customers that included the *New York Times*, *Wall Street Journal*, Bloomberg, the *Guardian*, Gawker, Univision, Meredith, Vice, Cars.com, Pandora, Spotify, and many others. We literally could "see" every user that came across those sites, and we helped hundreds of publishers use a DMP to decide if the users were "ETF portfolio readers," "Justin Bieber zealots," or "moms seeking to fuel the family."

Consistent with the "data-out" blueprint from Chapter 3, we built integrations to hundreds of outbound execution systems: desktop websites, mobile applications, video ad networks, social channels such as Facebook, CRM, programmatic exchanges, etc. Today, we hear a lot of talk about "real time," but the reality is that people move much more slowly than the Internet, and most systems are not nearly as real time as advertised. While we had the ability to transport our customers' data in near real time, many of our partners were a lot slower with data ingestion. This was akin to having Aroldis Chapman on the mound ready to pitch 105-mph fastballs but having to wait 24 hours between pitches.

While the issue was perhaps less important a few years ago, when channels were limited and e-commerce primarily occurred on a desktop computer, today it's more urgent: people move from device to device and channel to channel rapidly, and they expect updates to their online experiences in real time. We developed real-time segments that partners like Google and others could ingest within seconds of creation, so that someone abandoning a valuable online shopping cart could receive a customized ad showing the product she or he was considering mere seconds after leaving a website.

Part and parcel of activation is the concept of *not targeting* somebody at all. While marketers often conflate better targeting with greater outcomes in media campaigns, it is ironic that one of the best use cases for data-driven marketing is suppressing users from seeing advertising. When someone finally buys the shoes, or car, or flight, the advertiser has no incentive to continue targeting the person. In fact, every additional nickel spent on a converted user is a nickel wasted. Yet every channel and partner the advertiser uses will continue to engage that user with ads until the person's ID is updated with the information that a purchase has occurred. Over hours and days, the user who bought the shoes continues to see the same pair again and again. In the next several years, we will see a lot of energy in data "pipelining"—making sure that systems like ours that can process and update data and "pitch" it can be aligned in real time so that execution systems can "catch" what we are throwing. We'll talk more about how that might unfold in Chapter 7.

WHERE ARE MY PEOPLE AT?

We have a fondness for hip-hop music, which explains the unconventional name we gave one of our first data science reports: WAMPA. An acronym for Where (Are) My People At? the so-called WAMPA report was created at the behest of our clients that needed a way to visualize where their known customers spent their time online. Every month, we were capturing as many as 4 billion unique devices and online web visitors across the various publishers we worked with. With their permission, we could show marketers like L'Oréal USA the number of beauty consumers on their sites and apps at any given time.

We would show all of L'Oréal's brand buyers the density of their known customers, website visitors, and mobile app users across the publishers we worked with. L'Oréal's marketing team would get a sense of which sites had a high overlap of users against L'Oréal's core audience—and publishers would get invaluable exposure to L'Oréal's data-driven marketing team and agencies. Media properties that showed up big on the WAMPA report would be rewarded with more media dollars, and those that indexed even slightly would receive a greater consideration than sites that didn't show up at all. This was a win-win for L'Oréal and publishers that were seeking attention and spend from the world's fifth-largest marketer.

The report started out as a geeky bubble graph, and now it powers a remarkable data visualization tool found in a Salesforce product called Data Studio. Figure 4.3 depicts the user interface.

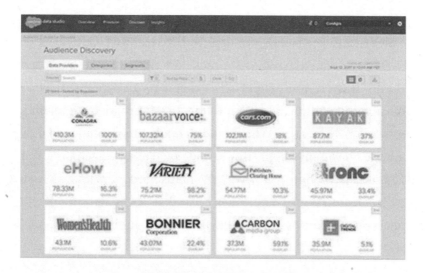

Figure 4.3 **The WAMPA—now called the "Audience Discovery Report"—maps the entirety of a marketer's first-party data against all the available second- and third-party data in the system. ConAgra uses this report to find out the overlap of its audience against data providers that it cares about, helping create more targeted media opportunities and custom data deals.**

The insights in the WAMPA report transformed media planning for our customers. Even today, marketers use survey-based metrics to shape their go-to-market strategies and depend on measurement companies like Nielsen and comScore to determine which media properties have the most reach among certain demographic groups. This is akin to traditional television planning, where marketers are accustomed to "buying into the demo"—making their purchasing decisions based on a television show's penetration into the important 18- to 54-year-old key demographic.[13] Broad measurement yardsticks like these move the needle on billions of dollars in broadcast and cable television spending, even though it's impossible to tell with precision just how many people tune in to watch. (Nielsen's panel works by surveying an incredibly tiny number of people who have their televisions hooked up to a box to determine which shows they watch. The company extrapolates to U.S. viewership numbers from that sample.[14])

The game changed as soon as companies could get exact counts of how many people were engaging with content, down to the amount of time they spent watching online videos or reading articles on a news site. Why shouldn't marketers demand to know exactly how many people they could reach at any given time and where those people were? WAMPA helps marketers know where their consumers are going, but in a way that drives investment and new opportunity for media destinations and publisher partners.

PERSONALIZATION: USING DATA TO BUILD GREAT CUSTOMER EXPERIENCES

Netflix has mastered the science of personalized show recommendations. As much as 75 percent of what Netflix users watch next comes from its algorithmic recommendations.[15] Over 35 percent of Amazon's revenue comes from sales of items suggested by its recommendation engine.[16] Pandora's Music Genome Project crunches hundreds of variables and creates incredibly satisfying playlists, learning as it goes so it can adapt to rapidly evolving consumer tastes.[17]

Marketers have been using available data for addressable marketing for years, but now they are starting to mine their own data and derive value from the information they collect from registrations, mobile applications, media performance, and site visitation, all of it enabled by a DMP. Many marketers are still just scraping the surface of what they can do, using data primarily for the targeting of addressable media. Some, however, are starting to deliver customer experiences that go beyond targeting display advertising by using data to shape the way consumers interact with their brands.

The case for personalization is robust. When the Watermark Group studied the cumulative stock performance of Forrester Research–rated "leaders" or "laggards" in customer experience, the results were staggering. During a period in which the S&P 500 grew by 72 percent, those focused on personalized experiences outperformed the market by 35 percent, and the laggards underperformed by 45 percent on average. That's a delta of nearly 80 percent in stock price performance between the winners and losers.[18]

Moreover, 89 percent of customers who have an unsatisfactory experience will leave a brand, according to a recent study; the cost of reacquiring a churned customer can run up to seven times the amount it took to win a new customer.[19] The stakes could not be higher for marketers and publishers looking to drive bottom-line performance. For many companies, whether they are marketing print or online subscriptions, promoting their content or selling products off the shelf, it's hard to justify to their CFOs the heavy costs associated with licensing platforms to gather the right data and use that data to drive relevant customer experiences. Yet when looking at big company priorities on multiple surveys, the desire to "create more relevant customer experiences" is right up there with "earn more revenue" and "increase profits." Why?

The simple answer is that customer experience has an enormous impact on both revenue and profitability. Giving new customers the right experience provides a higher probability of winning them, and giving existing customers relevant experiences reduces churn and creates opportunities to sell them more products, more often. When both top-line revenue and profitability can be driven through a single initiative, most CFOs start to invest and will continue to do so as results confirm the initial thesis.

Take the heavy user of a quick-service restaurant who dines several times a week and consistently transacts an over-average per-visit receipt. QSRs understand the impact that these valued customers have on the bottom line. These users provide a strong baseline of predictable revenue, are usually the first to try new product offerings, and respond to market-facing initiatives, such as discounting and couponing, which can strategically increase short-term receipts. Smart marketers should not be content to sit back and let this valuable segment remain stagnant or find new offerings from a competitive restaurant. The marketers must show these users that they are valued, ensure they retain or increase store visits, and keep them away from the hamburger chain next door. This can be as simple as offering a coupon for a regular customer's favorite order. Or it can be as complex as developing a mobile application that enables the customer to order food in advance and pick it as soon as it's ready.

The restaurant collects point-of-sale data and has authenticated user registration data from the mobile app, so it can now personalize the customer's order screen with the customer's most popular orders to shorten the mobile ordering experience. The application can offer special discounts to frequent diners for trying and rating new menu items. When on the road, the app can recommend other locations and direct the customer right to the drive-in window through popular map APIs. The possibilities are endless when you start to imagine how data can fuel your next customer interaction. Marketers and publishers are quickly leveraging their first-party data and aligning it with powerful applications that drive customer experience, increase profits, reduce customer churn, and boost lifetime value.

CASE IN POINT

Peugeot Tailors Content in Real Time to Lure Customers to the Showroom

When we first met with PSA Peugeot Citroën, the automobile company was struggling to drive consumers to the showroom. The company was ranked ninth globally in terms of production,[20] had recently taken a billion-Euro bailout, and was plotting a return to the U.S. market after an absence of nearly 20 years.[21] The company was marketing aggressively in Europe, its principal market, but seeing little in terms of increased foot traffic at dealerships.

(continued)

One executive we met with complained bitterly about her recent results with media: "We have multiple agencies. Every time we meet with them, their recommendation is to spend more money. So we raise our budget. But the only ones making any money are the agencies themselves. We just aren't selling enough cars." This is a common refrain among marketers, and it was the main concern for another top executive of PSA Groupe, when we met with him to discuss data-driven strategy for Peugeot during Dreamforce 2016. It is natural to equate increased marketing spend with improved sales results, but in a world where fickle consumers are hard to identify and convince, Peugeot knew it would take more than increased spending to reignite consideration for its brand.

Samir El Hammami, the manager of Peugeot Citroën's digital marketing team, had plenty of website data on people who came to PSA sites to browse inventory and use the custom car configuration tool to build and price auto models—but consumers visiting the site often left before they were fully engaged. Site "dwell times" were down, and most customers exited the website without requesting more information. Samir thought a more real-time application of people data could create stickier web experiences with the brands and ultimately result in more test drives. For most auto retailers, an in-person dealership visit was the ultimate signal of intent; drivers that Peugeot could persuade to move from site visitor to test driver were much more likely to purchase.

How could Samir use real-time people data to personalize the consumer's experience on mobile and web properties?[22] "My goal was to capture and analyze every interaction on the site—by car type, color, specification, and price—and use it to improve the number of consumers signing up for a test drive, which was my most critical performance metric," says Samir. "It hadn't really been done before, so it would require a big leap."

The challenge was connecting PSA's unique and granular customer segmentation (over 800 consumer microsegments, based on a combination of variables) with the most relevant content and delivering those experiences in the moment through the car company's custom content management system. This effort focused on the Peugeot, Citroën, and DS brands. We analyzed user behavior, activities, and events as they occurred in the users' browsers and computed microsegments and user affinities for various attributes—make, model, color, type, etc.—in real time. The challenge was one of speed: how could we compute all this information in a world where milliseconds mattered and browser-server round trips were too time-consuming? We met the challenge by putting the core affinity computation module into the browser itself and caching and updating it periodically, according to the frequency with which the user engaged with PSA's content.

In essence, we enabled PSA to "paint the page" to give the user on the other side of the screen an experience

(continued)

tuned perfectly to her interests. A data-mining technique called frequent pattern analysis identified patterns from a very large data set—in this case, the signals and attributes that resulted in an outcome of interest for Peugeot. Frequent pattern analysis is a great complement to A/B testing, a method many marketers already use, to compare the effectiveness of certain web pages or advertisements in a controlled experimental design. Here, frequent pattern analysis gave Peugeot the ability to test multiple hypotheses at once and reduce the amount of creative testing required so that the company could give its users a narrower, much more promising array of options.

OPTIMIZATION: FINDING EFFICIENCY AND EFFECTIVENESS IN ADDRESSABLE MEDIA

Everyone in media loves to quote the old John Wanamaker saw, "Half the money I spend on advertising is wasted—the trouble is, I don't know which half."[23] Sadly, what was true for this mid-nineteenth-century department store magnate remains true in today's digital media age. Working media dollars are still wasted, and perhaps in greater quantities than ever.

Although we have the ability to measure all addressable media at the device and channel level, the problem that most marketers face is an inability to measure their performance at the people level. As discussed in the "data-out" section earlier, if a marketer uses ten different addressable channels on a particular campaign (say, two DSPs, three social networks, e-mail, a mobile platform, search, and two direct buys), there are ten different IDs for the same exact user. Yes, you can set frequency controls (or caps) for every channel, but even limiting every partner to 20 impressions per user per month means exposing users to over 200 messages—far too many. A 2016 study by marketing automation provider Hubspot reported that 91 percent of people feel that advertising is even more intrusive than in years past.[24] If the vast majority of people feel overexposed to advertising, imagine how much worse we make it when we expose them to the same exact ad hundreds of times!

Kellogg Company was one of the earliest adopters of DMP technology and one of the first to drive a stake in the ground on frequency management. "We knew there were inefficiencies in digital. It was clear that we were over-serving ads to consumers, and it was also evident that much of our advertising spend was not getting enough user frequency to be effective," says Jon Suarez-Davis. "Although we were highly rigorous in terms of frequency capping our partners and bringing in partners like comScore for measurement, we knew we couldn't solve the problem without owning an identity infrastructure that could link user IDs together in a way that enabled a highly granular level of control." JSD brought us in to talk about how we were user-matching with the partners that Kellogg Company depended on, such as Yahoo!'s Brightroll,[25] a video advertising platform.

Anheuser-Busch InBev (ABI), another early adopter of data management technology from the CPG space, struggled with the same overages and underages. "One of the biggest challenges for CPG marketers is managing reach and frequency," says Jonny Silberman, director of digital strategy and innovation at ABI. "We want to reach as many consumers as possible, but at the right frequency of exposure. Too little exposure to our creative and consumers may not remember our brand, but too frequent exposures and we end up annoying them. The reach frequency challenge gets even harder as you enter the fragmented digital ecosystem."

Without an aerial view of people across the various devices and sites that Kellogg's and ABI were trying to reach them on, managing ad delivery was impossible. "We couldn't get a true measure of how many times we were reaching our consumer in the digital environment. Each of our publisher partners would come back to us with an average frequency for the campaign, but the data lived in silos. For example, if we only wanted to reach a consumer eight times per month with our Bud Light 'Dilly Dilly' campaign, we could set a frequency cap of eight with that publisher," Anheuser-Busch's Silberman explains. "At the end of the month Publisher A would come back with an average frequency of six, Publisher B would come back with a frequency of seven, and Publisher C would have a frequency of five. We thought we were doing a great job, maximizing our reach at the best frequency. But we were wrong. Once we combined the multiple touchpoints into a single consolidated view of the consumer, we realized that the same consumer was getting 18 ads instead of the 8 we planned for."

Consider the graph in Figure 4.4 that tracks what happens when customers see too many of the same ads. Marketers across every category and sector struggle with this dynamic.

In 2014, we partnered with Nielsen[26] and deployed our infrastructure in support of the "DMC II" initiative, tracking digital ads for a "digital media consortium," which included some of the biggest CPG companies in the world, such as Anheuser-Busch InBev,

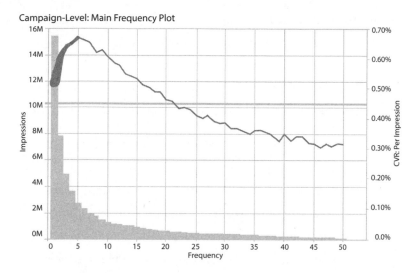

Campaign-Level: Main Frequency Plot

Figure 4.4 **A typical frequency analysis of a campaign showing the short tail of frequency, the optimal range of impressions that produces results, and the degradation of performance as consumers see too many of the same ads.**

Unilever, PepsiCo, and more. CPG companies, in their obsessive search for reach, knew they were being inefficient even in digital (Wanamaker's age-old "50 percent problem"). They wanted real data to validate their suspicions. After tracking hundreds of millions of dollars in digital spending, we found some eerie similarities.

Almost every frequency graph we looked at exhibited a similar dynamic:

- There was a *short tail* of impressions, where most budget was spent reaching users between one and three times per month—great for getting unique reach to net-new consumers, but not generating enough media exposure to really move the needle toward brand consideration or purchase. These were users who were underexposed.

- On the far end, there was a huge *long tail* of more than 20 impressions. These users were receiving far too many impressions every month. The overallocation of spend on these excess impressions resulted in huge inefficiency and possible brand diminishment for marketers.

- In the middle, there was always a *sweet spot* of frequency— usually somewhere between 3 and 20 impressions per user per month—that correlated most highly with conversion activity. When we mapped the advertising KPI data against frequency, we always found more clicks, completed video ad views, and coupon downloads within these impression bands.

While this data was not unexpected (of course, marketers are going to have a range of frequency by user), it was significant, because for the first time, we could actually *do* something about it. Marketers using our DMP could instruct their partners to stop serving ads to users who were overexposed to a campaign and target users who had not seen enough ads for the campaign to be effective. We could help marketers by diving into their conversion data and showing them the sweet spot where various users demonstrated the highest likelihood of converting. This new level of control was not just limited to "frequency-capping" users—it was a whole new way to think about the delivery of cross-channel messages and the ultimate attainment of the biggest prize of all: "right message, right place, right time."

For Anheuser-Busch InBev, this first step on the road to true delivery management was significant. "By simply connecting all of our digital media exposures together with a powerful technology we were able to finally get a full view of our consumer. Using our data management platform, we were able to decrease our over-delivery of impressions from 37 percent to 22 percent in only the first few months of implementing. This simple change improved consumer experience—and saved us over $1.5M in wasted impressions in the first few months of implementation," says Silberman.

Over the next several months, we worked with customers like Anheuser-Busch and Kellogg's to develop a playbook for marketers to enable them to achieve more granular control over message delivery. The methodology followed four key steps.

Step 1: Find the Sweet Spot

To build a frequency graph, marketers first have to pick their KPI. For brand marketers, sometimes clicks or completed views of a video ad can serve as proxies for brand consideration and engagement. For CPG companies, we routinely examined things like coupon downloads to show interest in a product; for travel advertisers, it might be an in-banner search for a specific flight. Once the key performance indicator is defined, the sweet spot becomes immediately apparent: there is a well-described frequency range where users engage within a certain amount of ad exposure. The more relevant the KPI, the more obvious the sweet spot becomes and vice versa—an important example of Principle #3 at work. In our large CPG study that tracked billions of impressions over three months, for example, it became clear that advertising effectiveness peaked between 3 and 20 monthly impressions and dropped precipitously thereafter (see Figure 4.5).

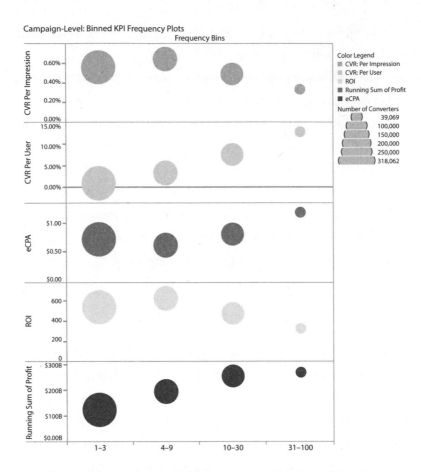

Campaign-Level: Binned KPI Frequency Plots

Figure 4.5 **How do you find the sweet spot for a brand? Data has the answers. In this typical frequency report, we show various key performance indicators by frequency bin. Note that users who viewed between 3 and 20 ads showed the highest conversion rates, highest return on investment, and largest profitability. Insights like these often transform a company's entire media strategy.**

Step 2: Eliminate the Long Tail

Every campaign has a "long tail" of frequency. In our research, the data showed a relentless pattern of disengagement after a user saw about 10 ad impressions over 30 days. Marketers could spend millions of dollars targeting the user with the eleventh, twelfth, or even one-hundredth ad and see only a negligible increase in performance.

This seemed obvious. All of our customers wanted to optimize their advertising delivery to only include effective impressions. By measuring engagement data against the number of viewed ads, we also stumbled upon a way to measure what we began to think of as the "now you are starting to piss me off" zone of delivery— the moment when you have seen a car or shoe ad so many times that you are no longer ignoring it, but actively hating the brand that keeps on sending it.

Tom once had a teacher who was fond of saying, "Numbers don't lie." His point was that real results from data build conviction, and conviction leads to more effective action. With data management platforms that connect user identity across multiple platforms, we can now use global delivery management, as outlined in Chapter 3, to instruct any addressable channel to suppress users across every system and screen. In other words, once a user has seen 10 ads, we can instruct the video and display advertising platforms to suppress them from targeting. By leveraging a DMP's vital "data-out" capability, we could effectively kill the long tail of ad exposure and ensure that brands like Kellogg's and Georgia-Pacific were not wasting precious media dollars bludgeoning customers who didn't want to hear from them any further. For Kellogg Company, this meant a savings of roughly 20 percent of its digital advertising budget, or nearly $25 million,[27] money the marketing team could invest in finding new customers.

Step 3: Nourish the Short Tail

Another interesting insight from studying hundreds of frequency analyses was the importance of the short tail of ad impressions: users who had been exposed to only one to three impressions over a period of 30 days. The bulk of media budgets usually goes toward reach, and the Internet is a wonderful tool for quickly exposing new users to a campaign message. In looking at the conversion data against users with a small amount of monthly ad exposure, however, we discovered that delivering only a few ads a month rarely moved the needle in terms of performance.

Digital consumers move quickly and are often task-oriented. We might take a few minutes at work between assignments to read an interesting article, and we often brush past an offer several times during a browsing session before stopping to engage with compelling content. This pattern presented itself over and over again when we looked at the data. Not enough ad impressions were actually worse than too many! Marketers were spending the majority of their working media dollars to expose new users to a campaign, but they were not giving the users enough ad impressions to bring them into brand consideration or get them to buy the product.

With data management, it's possible to take large groups of users and send that data into channels where you can instruct systems to pay more to ensure the users received the fourth or fifth ad exposure over time, bringing them into the frequency sweet spot where they are more likely to engage with a campaign. The math is straightforward: if you look at 100,000 users, and those who have seen four ad impressions have a 20 percent higher likelihood of engagement than users who have only seen three ads, a data-driven bidding strategy quickly emerges. Over time, we helped dozens of companies score their user segments and decide the specific cost of spending more to acquire them based on their current engagement with a campaign. Today, the prevalence of programmatic advertising (bidded systems) makes this tactic not only available, but a necessity for driving efficiency and effectiveness in addressable media spending. We called this "bidding users into the sweet spot."

Step 4: Tune for Recency

Yet another way to control delivery of messages is to think about recency, or the time period over which you actively send a message to consumers. Most brands retarget consumers who visit their website without purchasing, trying to recapture their interest and close a sale. Although an effective marketing tactic, retargeting has its detractors. It has been overused by many marketers, and as a result has become too closely associated with the "this pair of shoes is chasing me around the Internet" meme.

Delivering and suppressing advertising with recency data suggests that, at a certain point, seeing too many of the same ad becomes ineffective. Our chief data scientist, Yacov Salomon, and his team sought to solve this dilemma by adding a recency factor to our delivery frequency analysis (see Figure 4.6). The combination of both frequency and recency gave rise to several valuable new insights.

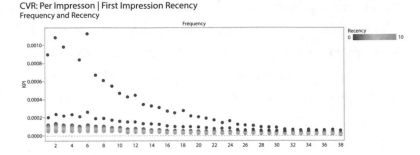

CVR: Per Impresson | First Impression Recency
Frequency and Recency

Figure 4.6 **Krux was an early pioneer in empowering companies to use data science to better understand how both the frequency and recency of delivered impressions impacted results.**

As Figure 4.6 shows, this particular campaign started tailing off after 12 days elapsed, and it failed to deliver any incremental value after about a month. This simple insight led to recommendations (e.g., "Stop retargeting users after two weeks") that resulted in hundreds of thousands of dollars in savings. The idea of pacing campaigns is not new: smart agencies have always "flighted" campaigns over weeks or months to correspond to different weekdays, holidays, or other important timelines. What's new with recency analysis is the ability to *validate* the performance and cost benefits of pacing, as well as the granular ability to control pacing across hundreds of different media partners from a single interface.

MAINTAINING A PEOPLE-BASED VIEW OF FREQUENCY

The synthesis of these techniques for coordinating frequency and recency has come to be known as global delivery management— the ability to reach across all channels, set specific instructions for serving or suppressing exposure, and actively control messaging at the segment level. This functionality is only available to marketers who can reconcile people identity across different device IDs and keys and activate them in external systems.

As outlined in Chapter 2, many systems think of the users we just described as IDs: online cookies, mobile IDs, different browser identities, or even over-the-top device IDs. With nearly four distinct devices and browsers for every person, a frequency graph showing a user with only two unique ad exposures might actually mean that someone with four devices has seen your campaign eight times. You can't optimize what you can't count, and you can't count what you don't see. Nailing the sweet spot of customer engagement according to our four-step strategy requires a central activation mechanism that reliably sees, tracks, and reconciles the multiple versions of you.

We live in an age in which just about every piece of media exposure data we can capture adds to our understanding of consumers. We also live in an era where many of the ads we buy online are never seen by actual people. It is the kind of 50 percent measurement problem that would make John Wanamaker happy to have lived in the 1800s. Today's online display ads are often shown "below the fold" and never seen unless a user scrolls down to the bottom of a page. Sometimes the ads are in view for a fraction of a second before the user skips somewhere else.

More notoriously, they're frequently "viewed" by robots, who cannot and will never book a family vacation or walk down the cereal aisle at Kroger. There are bad actors in the advertising ecosystem who use the programmatic exchanges outlined in Chapter 1 to extract millions of dollars in online advertising budgets from unsuspecting marketers. Marketers began to understand the scale of the scam around 2013. In essence, the scammers create millions of fake users, deploy bots to stand in for real human beings, and skim money from budgets set aside for programmatic advertising. The scam, however, presents another invaluable use case for DMPs: use suppression to *not* send an impression to a user if you suspect it's a bot.

This combination of nonviewability and nonhuman traffic[28] can result in wasted media spend.[29] The solution to this problem is to partner with vendors that can measure and report on viewability and also identify clicks and views that didn't come from people at all. At Krux we worked closely with vendors such as Integral Ad Science, Moat, and comScore to add a viewability layer to campaigns so our frequency analyses could be based on people who had actually seen an ad. We accumulated the IDs of users we knew to be nonhuman and actively suppressed them from inclusion in campaigns—savings that often added up to as much as 5 percent of total spend, or millions of dollars per year for larger advertisers.

INSIGHTS: DATA BACK IN AGAIN

If marketers are going to channel their inner Amazon, they need to know as much as possible about their customers, and every granular bit of data is a clue to be stitched together with others in the relentless pursuit of new ideas to drive the business forward. "Data in" is the method by which we construct user profiles from everything we know. "Data out" is the method by which we find people across the channels, surfaces, and systems they visit. Analytics—"data back in"—is the way we look at user engagement across channels and enrich our understanding of users. Combining the data inherent in all three approaches is what gives today's marketer the ability to meld art into the science of data-driven marketing.

Marketers are feverishly putting together customer data platforms (CDPs) and data lakes to store and refine their people data. These are repositories of their first-party data. We've worked with big airline marketers like JetBlue, which can easily put together enough purchase data to distinguish leisure travelers from business travelers, and also which likely has a good grasp on the right cadence and messaging for an e-mail campaign. But what if the marketer wanted to take all of its recent campaign data promoting its airport club lounges and compare it against the beacon data it collected to see how many of the recipients of the ad actually made a recent visit? What if the marketer wanted to slice that data and compare visitors with an existing membership and new members? Wouldn't it be interesting to know how much a membership impacted the total lifetime value of a frequent flier? These are the questions that can be answered only with technology powerful enough to probe data sets actively maintained in a single logical space.

Data-rich marketers like airlines have enormous data on their customers, which requires lots of data integration. Their challenge is building the right filters on the data to separate the truly valuable signals from the noise and construct algorithms that ask smart questions and produce actionable answers. What are the truly important signals? Does decreasing the fare by $100 on a popular business route increase demand from high-value frequent business travelers, or does it artificially increase demand from occasional travelers, filling seats too early and too cheaply, ultimately reducing profit? Marketers with loads of data are plumbing the depths to answer these kinds of business questions, and now they can attach rich sets of media analytics and device data to understand how the investments they make in cross-channel advertising move the needle.

Data-poor marketers have the opposite challenge: with little first-party customer data, they need to enrich their data lakes with many different signals to understand the identity and behavior of their customers. How cold does it have to be to increase sales of soup over its weekly average? What is the impact of increased advertising to drive demand in the wake of a storm? What kinds of recipes do people make during different seasons, and how many of the different ingredients does my company own?

To promote Bear Naked Custom Made Granola, Kellogg's asked IBM's Watson to look at the chemical composition of 10,000 different recipes from *Bon Appetit* to find ingredients that blended together seamlessly. This big data back end was integrated with the Bear Naked Custom Made Granola website, which enabled consumers to blend their own specialty granola from dozens of different ingredients. During the process, "Chef Watson" automatically scored the "flavor synergy" of the custom mix based on its analysis. Users chose custom package graphics to "name and claim" their special blend. An integration into Salesforce's commerce engine let users purchase directly from the site, with the custom granola landing on their doorsteps a few days later. One assumes that Kellogg's will use the data from thousands of orders to make decisions on which prepackaged blends to put into the local Piggly Wiggly.

Big data–enabled analytics is driving real change. Imagine if Kellogg's had richer insights into its purchase data 10 years ago, when consumers were just starting to turn from traditional packaged goods to more natural foods? Perhaps the company would have caught the Greek yogurt craze and bought a company like Chobani or Oikos before it turned into a billion-dollar business.[30]

Even marketers with relatively sparse data are finding new ways to get a competitive edge with media analytics. Every click, video view, and impression is a valuable signal. Marketers that can associate what happens with their campaigns at the people level can use those insights to gain competitive advantage. The power of people data can be used in real time, for example, to mine insights during an online campaign. Think about the process that creative agencies go through to test various messages. Still today, much of that work involves real-life focus groups and small, self-selected panels of people. The process is highly manual, taking days or weeks to assemble the panels, expose them to advertising, get the results, and undertake an analysis. Agencies have started to evolve that process with faster testing online—building multiple variables of an ad and testing them rapidly in small online campaigns. Today, with the ability to microsegment customers and activate campaigns for them almost immediately, every marketer with a data management platform has the ability to test an unlimited number of assumptions and receive instantaneous results.

CASE IN POINT

A&E Discovers the Power of the Mobile Nudge to Drive Tune-In

A particularly powerful example of "data back in" is the History Channel's tune-in campaign for *Vikings*. *Vikings* was an immediate hit when it debuted in 2013, drawing over 6 million viewers. A&E, owner of the History Channel, caught lightning in a bottle and was eager to leverage the success of the debut stabilize its viewership base, and,

(continued)

most importantly, drive people to tune in on the weeknight when the show aired.

Because Krux could time-stamp every addressable interaction and align that data back to individual users, we detected some trends in media performance data that immediately made sense. We noticed a spike in engagement on mobile devices prior to the show airing on Thursday nights. These were people at home on tablets and mobile phones settling in for "appointment television." *Vikings* was a show that viewers wanted to watch live rather than record and watch later, a phenomenon enjoyed only by a few blockbusters such as *Game of Thrones* and *Westworld*.

We also noticed that people who had seen at least three website banner ads for *Vikings* were much more likely to engage with mobile tune-in ads on the night of the show. We dubbed this effect the "mobile nudge." The tactic was simple: focus on people likely to watch *Vikings* and engage them with display creative all week, building anticipation for the show, and then switch to mobile ads to capture people who were at home and remind them when the show was airing. This simple channel-switching tactic created massive uplift in tune-in for *Vikings* and helped A&E capture and hold greater numbers of *Vikings* fans. Most critically, it enhanced viewership on the actual air date of the show, increasing ratings, which had a follow-on effect.

Without data back in and the insights that the data offers, even seemingly simple addressable tactics are hard to see—and impossible to validate.

CHAPTER 5

MAKING IT REAL FOR YOUR ORGANIZATION

All the data management capabilities in the world cannot bring a company to the promised land of data-driven marketing. Over the years, we have seen hundreds of companies declare their commitment to using data to drive marketing strategy and invest in the people and processes required to make it stick. In all cases, it requires clear leadership from the top and the middle. And at the beginning of the journey, it just takes a reason to believe.

"There is no shortage of acronyms in modern marketing," says Anheuser-Busch's Jonny Silberman. "You have RFP (request for proposal), DMP (data management platform), PMP (private marketplace), CDP (consumer data platform). It can go on and on. For us, the most important was RTB, which for us didn't stand for 'Real-Time Bidding,' but rather 'Reason to Believe.' That is what we needed to give our senior management team to get buy-in for our data-driven journey, and we needed to do it fast. Once we had our RTB, it kicked off a revolution."

It's time to turn our attention away from technical and strategic considerations and dive fully into the much harder part of organizational adoption. In this chapter, we consider the stakeholders in your company who must come together to create a data center of excellence; an engagement maturity model that can help you determine where your organization is living on the continuum of data-driven capability; and five pitfalls to avoid on the path to data-driven excellence. We've seen well-resourced companies with ample staff, time, and money fumble when it comes to the implementation of their vision. We've also seen companies with fewer resources but far greater discipline successfully develop a high-functioning apparatus for data-driven marketing. The difference maker is people: the operator who can think laterally and creatively about how to marshal the energies of the organization, how to avoid the pitfalls, and how to drive implementation and persuasively communicate its results. Master these methods, and you can transform not just your company, but your career.

DEVELOPING A DATA CENTER OF EXCELLENCE

Sometimes we encounter a marketer or media company that has licensed a DMP but is struggling to harness full value from it. We recently talked to a customer with this issue who told us, "We have the Ferrari in the garage, but nobody knows how to drive it, so every time we take it out for a spin, we crash." It's a common refrain among companies seeking to excel in data-driven marketing with the machinery, but not the organizational readiness and structure, to extract its benefits.

A serious team approach is required to build what we call the data center of excellence (DCOE). The DCOE is usually composed of internal folks from the media, analytics, and IT teams; smart consultants for change management; systems integration partners; and agencies. The companies that adopt such an approach reap near-term value in the beginning stages of their journey, which more than funds all their subsequent efforts.

We think of the pillars of organizational adoption as *people, process,* and *technology.* There is no partial credit: getting one or two of those right and the other wrong leads to failure. The greatest data technology in the world falls down without the right people behind it. The most well-thought-out and rigorous process fails to scale without the right technology. And of course, the best people in the world are ineffective without the right habits and processes in place to coordinate their efforts.

It starts with people. When looking across the hundreds of DMP implementations we have supported, the companies that get value the most quickly have implicitly or explicitly created a DCOE that defines data strategy holistically and assigns ownership clearly across key stakeholders in the organization.

Figure 5.1 describes how progressive companies organize for data-driven success, establishing key disciplines in media, analytics, and marketing technology (IT).

Media

Whether it's the CMO managing cross-channel ad spending or the chief revenue officer of a media company charged with yield optimization across various media offerings, the media team is usu-

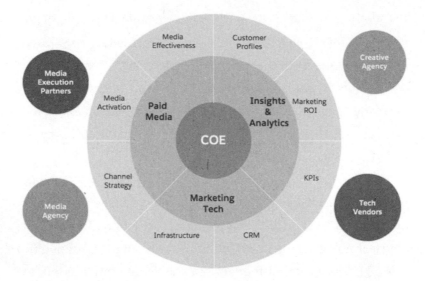

Figure 5.1 **The power of a data center of excellence radiates from key stakeholders in the media, analytics, and IT functions with a cohesive strategy across a broad base of partners.**

ally the first group crying out for a coherent data strategy and the tools to make it work. The media team has very specific needs and KPIs around data. Typically, the team is looking for better audience discovery, more precise segmentation, tools to enable efficiency in media spending (or sales), the ability to get fast insights to support optimization opportunities, and the capacity to integrate with the tools currently in use.

Media has been a hot growth area in technology, and today's media personnel have experimented with a variety of different tools over the last decade as advertising has moved from the network era to today's multichannel programmatic environment. We often see media teams lead evaluations of data technology and serve as a hub for colleagues from analytics, IT, and its associated CRM counterparts to shape the organizational data initiative. Media is also the fastest path to ROI: for advertisers, it offers the ability to optimize and reduce rogue or inefficient spending; for publishers, it is the ability to improve monetary yield through better audience segmentation.

Analytics

Today's analytics departments come to the table with a great deal of enthusiasm for data centralization and closer connections to the media team, which is a rich source of user intent data. Many teams are challenged to combine the rich, structured data they are getting from CRM, commerce, and offline sales data with newly available, fast-flowing media and unstructured data. It would be ideal for the automobile retailer to connect online advertising exposure data, e-mail data, and location data in a single place to understand how advertising impacted dealership visits, but such data most often remains siloed and hard to connect. Analytics stakeholders see great opportunity in a DCOE approach that mandates participation from across the organization.

Like their media counterparts, analytics teams have embraced many new technologies over the years for various use cases, and they continually seek ways to make their insights easily digestible to management and other stakeholders. Yet we continue to see data flow shackled by old modalities, accessible through structured data warehouses that require long wait times and different query languages to access. Modern analysts need built-in dashboards that can make the most common reports broadly accessible. They also need flexibility to draw from a single source of organizational data to run custom reports, perform modeling, and drive deeper levels of analysis.

Analysts are concerned with uncovering richer insights, using data to identify better customer experiences, a model customer lifetime value, the propensity to purchase, and richer segmentation. They are eager to connect this data with that of the media team to provide better planning, optimization strategies, and measurement.

IT

Much has been made about the convergence of the CMO and CIO functions, and for good reason. The modern CMO cannot execute a data strategy without being conversant in the technology tools and tactics required to execute it. In a perfect world, the role of chief data officer (CDO) would oversee the functional areas of both IT and CRM and serve as the ideal partner to join colleagues in media and analytics in a DCOE. Because not every company has made that leap, we often see both groups represented as IT.

They are charged with making sure that the vision of the media and analytics teams conforms to the overall corporate technology strategy, that it aligns the investment goals of the group with the corporate technology and infrastructure budgets, and, most critically, that the project proceeds with strong data governance, privacy rules, and existing security protocols.

To succeed, IT groups must serve as strong stewards of their customer data. As we discussed in Chapter 1, this entails ensuring user privacy, trust, and transparency while allowing for data collection to enable better customer experience; protecting customers from breaches of their personal and financial data; and keeping abreast of international and local laws to ensure their data collection practices are in compliance. In Chapter 1, we outlined some changes resulting from GDPR that are especially relevant to matters of consumer privacy and data usage in the European Union. Once that backbone is in place, IT stakeholders will need to understand how new systems will connect with existing infrastructure, how the systems will be able to scale and grow with the company, and what levels of control and access accompany the technologies used to serve the DCOE goals.

In the continually evolving world of consumer devices, the ever-growing pools of data available for capture, and the evolving regulatory and legal landscape for protecting user data, IT's full participation is a necessary condition for the successful construction of a DCOE. We know that no successful DCOE rollout has happened without the full integration and support of the technology group.

A successful data center of excellence must attend to the interests and objectives of multiple stakeholders, shown in Table 5.1.

The Vendor Ecosystem

While the core DCOE team is critical, data-driven transformation cannot unfold within just the four walls of the organization. Every marketer and media company we have worked with comes to the table with a wide array of agencies, technology vendors, consultants, and partners. Key vendors must have a seat at the table and be given strong incentives to adopt a more data-centric methodology.

We were recently in a quarterly business review with one of our clients, a large CPG beverage company, and its media agency. Data on our platform revealed some interesting new results on media exposure and website visitation. Contrary to the agency's strategy, the overwhelming proportion of positive media interactions

Table 5.1 **Criteria for a Successful Data Center of Excellence**

Media	Analytics	IT	CRM
Integrations: Has to work with my stack	**Insights:** Tell me things I don't already know	**Security:** Does it comply with my policies?	**Onboarding:** I need an environment that brings my known customers online
Efficiency: Must make what I'm doing now better	**CX:** What are the insights that drive better CX? What makes my customers like me?	**Governance:** Can it be managed easily as it scales?	**POS data:** I want to put my sales data and other OL attributes to work
Optimization: Must enable me to optimize as I get insights	**Modeling:** I need data to power propensity models and user scoring	**Control:** I want to control permissions and access in a highly granular way	**E-mail:** How do I make my e-mail campaigns better?
Discovery: I need to find unique reach	**Personas:** How can this help me refine what I already know about my customers?	**Scale:** Can I break it? What's under the hood?	**CX:** How can I use my CRM data to create better personalized experiences?
Omnichannel: I need to activate insights across everything	**Lifetime value/ ROI:** I want a "golden record" of all my customers who have an LTV score	**Extensibility:** How does it play with my existing systems—and support future bolt-ons?	**Offboarding:** How can I enrich my CRM data with online attributes and behavior?

(clicks, site visits, and video views) came from women and older men. Because the agency was only measuring success by penetration into males aged 21–49 (the "demo"), the agency considered its campaign a failure—even though in-store sales were increasing! In other words, the agency was successful even though it wasn't achieving the measurement metric it defined. The beverage company was happy to have engaged older drinkers. Why was success measured in a way that discounted the power of the company's older, wealthier, and more engaged demographic? The agency folks were hanging their heads over a lawyerly issue of metrics definition when they should have been crowing about shared success.

Clearly, the availability of data drives the need for new ways to measure, and in this case, to prescribe a new way for a media agency to measure results. That same company used an online audience verification tool to measure the amount of invalid traffic that clicked on its ads and visited its website—but could not suppress those visitors until it became more sophisticated in the use of its data management platform. Once the company matured, some of its vendors balked at the decrease in volumes of the agency's campaigns, after a nearly 20 percent reduction of committed spending.

Newly available data required the vendor, a demand-side platform, to change the way it engaged with a more sophisticated marketer. In both instances, the agency and vendor would have expected these changes if they understood the strategy earlier and were more fully enrolled as partners in the COE. We have seen this dynamic play out again and again. When there is a cross-functional team built around data with the right goals and metrics, less money is wasted agreeing on yardsticks and more investment is spent reaching customers.

CAPABILITY MATURITY MODEL

Data-driven transformation unfolds along a continuum. Even within the most advanced centers of excellence, success depends on a number of factors. Of course, it starts with people, process, and technology, but a capability model evolves to include collecting data and setting goals grounded in the data you collect. We see successful transformation strategies aligned to five common areas of measurement: *goals, people, process, data,* and *tools*.

- **Goals.** Are your business objectives clearly stated, and are they grounded in the ability to measure them with data?

- **People.** Have you aligned your digital transformation to a unified DCOE approach with the right people, proper coordination across groups, and executive alignment?

- **Process.** Have you committed to a process driven by a clear, stepwise approach to transformation, with crystal-clear, metric-driven KPIs for each step of the journey?

- **Data.** Will your decisions be made and action taken based on data from all available sources?

- **Tools.** Finally, will your systems have the autonomy necessary to enable your data team to focus on higher-order tasks, such as analysis and insights, rather than button-pushing execution?

The right people executing against a goals-driven strategy, basing their decisions on data, building success incrementally through scalable tools that enable true strategy—this is, in our experience, the most effective path forward. The key is to develop competency in these five areas and grow those capabilities over time.

As part of our research, we surveyed over 40 large marketers and media companies that have undergone, or are in the process of undergoing, data-driven marketing transformation. Looking at the progress of the three companies from beginning to end, we saw three distinct categories: informal, organized, and optimized. Taken together, they define the three stages of a capability maturity model for data-driven performance (see Table 5.2).

Table 5.2 **Informal, Organized, and Optimized Stages of Data-Driven Operation**

Dimension	Stage 1	Stage 2	Stage 3
Goals	Business decisions are not yet data driven. Client has unclear business objectives.	Data is used in accomplishing certain business objectives, yet some objectives are ambiguous.	Business objectives are clearly stated with data as a principal component of the client's business goals.
People	Ad hoc responsibility for data analysis with inconsistent skill levels.	Formalized roles and responsibilities (i.e., data monetization lead).	Clear coordination across groups or centralized center of excellence.
Process	Relevant, documented processes (people work inside process, rather than outside).	Streamlined processes focused on decisions, coordinated activity across the enterprise.	Fast-paced decision-making calendar and metric-driven process initiation triggers.
Data	All relevant behavioral data is collected and securely stored.	Decisions are made and action taken based on online and offline data collected.	Data powers stand-alone revenue streams.
Tools	Process controls and stable infrastructure.	Support incorporation of second-party data in campaign design and analysis.	Third parties own day-to-day execution systems and data team focuses on analysis and insight.

Stage 1: Informal

In this early stage, goals are less clear. Business decisions are not 100 percent data driven because not enough useful data has flowed through the organization. There are usually a few stake-holders running analytics, but useful insights do not flow through the entire organization to drive change, and the level of skill among people varies. From a data perspective, there is relevant behavior data flowing into the platform from easy-to-capture sources such as web analytics tools and digital advertising pixels, but offline data remains stuck in its own silo. Most companies at this early stage have built process controls around the data and have a stable infra-structure in place (usually a DMP) to manage data capture. The companies in Stage 1 are ready to create a DCOE, execute against a road map of use cases aligned with ROI goals, and start sharing data across the organization.

Stage 2: Organized

Most of the clients we work with fall into this broad category of "organized" companies that are leveraging data for certain pur-poses, but have yet to fully exploit all the data-driven possibilities within reach. They have clear goals in place for certain use cases ("Achieve 15 percent reduction in wasteful ad spend"), but have less formalized goals in other areas ("Get better at understanding where customers go"). They have established some key roles and responsibilities within their company by assigning a media lead or analytics lead, but have yet to fully embrace the DCOE to share data and coordinate its access and use across silos. From a pro-cess perspective, they have managed to streamline certain functions and are starting to coordinate activity across the enterprise. (For example, if a new purchase segment became available, the media agency would be notified automatically and given the ability to optimize a media campaign with new data). At the organized stage, the company has centralized most if not all of its data in a single system, combining offline CRM with addressable online data, and sometimes it even has access to new data sources, such as second-party data relationships with key partners offering some kind of differentiated advantage.

Stage 3: Optimized

There are a handful of companies that have truly embraced data transformation across the five key areas, and their efforts have borne fruit. Meredith, Adidas, L'Oréal USA, Turner, Pandora, ABI, and a few others leaned in early and sustained their investments and executive commitment to data-driven excellence over a period of three to five years.

They espoused clear business objectives centered on the use of data to transform their relationships with customers. For example, when L'Oréal USA's CMO Marie Gulin celebrated the incredible growth of mobile IDs in her data platform with her team, it was not about capturing as much data as possible. It was, rather, part of a plan to build deeper, more relevant conversations with customers by driving adoption of the company's Makeup Genius app, which correlated to e-commerce sales.

Pandora went beyond just capturing and activating data to creating entire new revenue streams with its first-party data. Today, Pandora has a thriving business helping advertisers with precision targeting using data not found elsewhere. Many of the advertisers opened up their data to a broader ecosystem of partners and vendors. They maintain ownership over their data and set their own data strategy, but they have given their partners and agencies access to data as a means of achieving a common lexicon for audience segmentation and KPIs.

These companies all embraced the data COE framework early and did the hard work of collaborating with technology, legal, and executive stakeholders to ensure success. Each was dedicated to a process based on facts that the data uncovered, no matter how much the results challenged the status quo.

THE FIVE COMMON PITFALLS ON THE PATH TO DATA-DRIVEN EXCELLENCE

After supporting the implementation of DMPs hundreds of times, we've learned a lot about what makes companies successful in the execution of their data-driven strategies. But we probably learned more from companies that initially failed on their journey. There are five big pitfalls that a company can encounter as it pursues data-driven transformation.

Pitfall #1: Absence of Clear Goals for Data Transformation

It sounds obvious, but even the world's biggest companies have fallen prey to embarking on data transformation without clear goals in place. Once Company A signs a big license deal with a software vendor and announces a grand strategy of digital modernization, it is tempting for Company B to follow with a technology investment of its own. The world moves fast. Nobody wants to be left behind, or to be the CMO who failed to see and act on a strategic trend.

We wish we could count on only one hand the number of times we have seen a big company jump on the technology bandwagon, expecting transformation to come on the heels of smart software investment. But "software as a service" is just that—a service—and great tools need to be deployed with clear, measurable goals and tied directly to the company's business strategy. Any business that licensed our DMP could claim that the business "needed better tools for targeting online consumers." In fact, this describes 100 percent of our customer base. It was the customers who approached the undertaking with more specific, measurable objectives (e.g., "I want to increase the amount of time customers spend on my website by 20 percent," or "I want to increase my conversion rates on video advertising by 30 percent through more granular customer segmentation") who always achieved far greater value.

Part of getting this right is making sure the correct stakeholders in the organization are in control of the process. If the software buying decision is being made by the IT team, but the primary use case for the software is to get more media efficiency, then there is a disconnect. (IT teams know as much about advertising tactics as media teams know about writing JavaScript.) In short, the right team must go into a digital transformation project with a clear set of KPIs that are tied to the health of the business. Those initial goals should start with garnering positive ROI from the software and then should align to the overall business strategy.

Leveraging technology for digital transformation without clear goals is akin to buying a truckload of lumber, nails, and hammers and hiring 20 carpenters without an architectural plan. What are the success factors needed to avoid this pitfall and create a clear, ROI-focused vision for digital transformation?

- **Align goals to use cases.** If a business goal for the company is "Reduce customer acquisition costs," then that should be aligned to a data transformation use case such as "Refine customer segmentation to increase conversion rates on targeted campaigns." Never pursue data-driven use cases that do not have a compelling and measurable outcome. "Know more about my online consumer" is an important but squishy goal. "Capture engagement data to better understand video media investment in key segments to increase conversion rates," in contrast, is a measurable, achievable goal.

- **Build a KPI framework.** You cannot track the effectiveness of your data transformation without a clear performance framework, and having KPIs to align with is paramount. This can be simple, "Expand addressable customer segments from 10 to 100 over the first three months," or more complex, "Reduce nonhuman traffic in digital advertising from 35 percent to 5 percent over the first six months, saving $1.5 million." Your team needs clear benchmarks, and you need to align your work to clear metrics to prove that transformation works, so the investment can continue.

- **Align data and business goals.** Data transformation can get into the weeds quickly, and goals like "better segmentation" might not necessarily snap to the success metrics that the executive team has put into place. Any time you can equate a data goal to a higher-order business goal, you increase the power of the project and win more executive alignment and budget. "We will increase the effectiveness of marketing by 15 percent by driving customer acquisition through more efficient digital channels, rather than expensive traditional channels."

Pitfall #2: Lack of a Formal Owner

Just like companies that forget to set clear goals ("We are going to build a house"), the company that goes into a project without an owner (the general contractor) is similarly doomed. Over the years we have seen key stakeholders at many different companies try to grab the reins of a data-driven initiative without the right executive alignment to be successful. An example is when a really strategic and capable media executive implements a data management solution to make advertising better, but this executive operates in a silo with no alignment to the analytics team tasked with tracking and measuring customer-facing success metrics. Or this can be a company that buys a new marketing technology and immediately farms out the project to its agency, which has little incentive to train and enable its cross-client teams on a solution specific to one client.

In this case, there are clear goals for the project ("Gain efficiency in our media spending with better control over frequency," as an example), but no real owner on the line for driving in-house adoption. As we've discussed, making the leap from "media driven" to "consumer driven" is a mindset and organizational approach that needs multiple stakeholders and executive alignment to succeed. It cannot live in a single department, and it cannot be farmed out to an agency and be transformative.

It's like taking care of a house: people who own their own homes are willing to invest time and money to fix them up and maintain them. Renters have little incentive to invest for the long term and will only do what's expedient at the moment. Data transformation requires true ownership, a champion who believes in the mission and can align the work with strategy and goals with the support of the executive team.

There are three ways to avoid the tragedy of good intentions that lack of formal ownership brings:

- **Hire a chief digital officer.** This can be a chief "experience" officer or even "customer" officer, who has responsibility for data-driven transformation. The CDO should be a high-energy performer who can align data initiatives to clear business goals and be responsible for creating a data center of excellence.

- **Create a data center of excellence.** Establish a formal executive steering committee that serves as the founding group of the DCOE. While there can be a single owner such as the chief digital officer responsible for the overall health and progress of reporting data transformation, the real "owner" needs to be a group of like-minded stakeholders across the organization, sharing resources and accountable to the goals.

- **Train and enable.** Help your agencies and partners take ownership of the tools used for data transformation. We've seen several big data efforts stumble when companies fail to transfer their strategy and skills to an external partner, such as a media agency. Ownership isn't just about setting strategy and buying tools and farming the work out to a consultant or agency. Taking ownership means training and enabling your partner ecosystem and holding those partners accountable for the same KPIs you have established for success.

Pitfall #3: Operating in a Silo

Over the years we have seen many examples of a single group within a larger organization achieve meaningful success with data initiatives but then fail to achieve the full transformation that was within reach because the group was stuck in its own operational silo. This can happen when the analytics team is getting great insights about users from a data management platform but not sharing the user scores with the media team for better activation. It can be when the media team is getting amazing media performance data but failing to share that data with the IT team members, who are building propensity models in their data warehouse. It can also happen when operators leave a company without transferring their knowledge to others, and data transformation walks out the door with them.

This can be painful and ironic, given that data transformation is, at its core, meant to eliminate data silos and to bring about transformation by aligning an organization's data and people toward a set of shared goals. Recently, we saw an example where after several years of successfully executing a digital strategy, the media team of a large company lost its budget for DMP software. The executives at the company were not aware of the need for the investment and assumed the agency could do it better.

How can this be avoided?

- **Treat data like an asset and trade it.** How can the media department get the CRM department to help fund a DMP? The media team can help deepen user profiles to make e-mail targeting better. Similarly, the analytics team can collaborate with the IT department on enriching the data science team's lifetime propensity models with user-level media interaction and online conversion data. Data is a currency. Use it to treat your cross-departmental stakeholders to data that also drives their success.

- **Align and combine budgets.** If people aren't paying for the expensive software another team is using, then they have little incentive to use it. When it comes to software tools that drive data transformation, the tools can never be procured in a silo. People naturally align with their own work goals, and no amount of goodwill is going to win you enough volunteers to join in a data center of excellence. When goals and budgets are shared, it's in everyone's interests to pursue outcomes together.

This seems like pure common sense, until you get to larger companies where multimillion-dollar initiatives can remain siloed in a single department under one executive.

Pitfall #4: Boiling the Ocean

A fate worse than operating in a single silo and doing too little with data transformation might be the opposite: trying to do too much at once. Whether it's software or consulting services being sold, you can be sure the solution is being marketed as the ultimate tool for transforming a company's entire business. Media is going to get more efficient, messaging is going to be more personalized, and insights are going to be delivered that can transform the organization at its core. All very true, but like the board game Othello, concepts such as these take a minute to learn—but a lifetime to master.

This situation can arise when a company strives for technical perfection before activation, such as mandating that every single type of data be integrated into a DMP before using the data for activation (frequently at the behest of IT groups, whose worries about data quality sometimes stand in the way of practical, quick wins). We have seen companies strive for such excellence, waiting months to integrate store beacon data into their data platform until they activate, when they could have been using data for retargeting site visitors within days. Data transformation is a process, and low-hanging fruit must be plucked rapidly to show quick wins and revenue opportunities that more than pay for future bolting and tightening.

Another example of boiling the ocean is when we see clients jump right into the most complex data use cases, requiring high levels of expertise and data integration. For example, one client wanted to begin with building cross-channel journeys (which we will cover further in the next chapter) that required months of historical data from multiple vendors and channels. Simply starting with suppressing past purchasers to eliminate the long tail covered in Chapter 4 would have been a fast, measurable, and much more achievable win.

To avoid the pitfall of trying to transform too quickly, you should strive to adopt an agile and iterative approach oriented around very specific outcomes:

- **Target quick wins.** The best data transformations are self-funding, incrementally producing ROI through each new use case. Quick wins build initial support for the larger vision and instill confidence that the ultimate goal of digital transformation can be achieved. Start with simple, provable use cases such as retargeting or suppression and build consensus for increasing budgets and workforce.

- **Create a road map.** Be ambitious, but stage it over time. Ask your teammates to identify the three things they want to achieve this year. Successful clients will pick two or three main initiatives and relentlessly drive toward them. For Kellogg's, it started with suppressing users who were seeing too many ads ($20 million in annual savings), and continued with suppressing nonhuman traffic from the company's advertising (another $3 million in savings). After getting these immediate wins, executives aligned quickly around the transformation plan, and they now had the experience to pursue more ambitious goals.

- **Stack-rank your goals.** Every use case has its own benefit (ROI) and its corresponding level of difficulty.

Changing your entire segmentation strategy is difficult, requiring multiple stakeholders and alignment across the organization, and its value is hard to map to revenue. But using website analytics data to target consumers on display advertising is simple, fast, and easy to A/B-test.

Pitfall #5: Failure to Anticipate Risk

Data transformation is hard work and, like all such endeavors, is fraught with risk. Look at today's agency landscape, where the Mad Men of advertising have been caught flat-footed by digital transformation, or traditional publishing, in free fall as over 90 percent of incremental ad dollars find their way to the "triopoly" of advertising platforms owned by Google, Amazon, and Facebook.

Data transformation often requires rewriting old rules, creating new yardsticks, and challenging the successes of the past. Newly acquired data must be integrated into existing frameworks, and process change must take place organizationally and with partners. Here are two ways to get a head start on risk mitigation:

- **Identify data fit and integrate.** What are the areas where newly acquired data can be put to work in existing structures? Is an agency partner still selecting data using old media demographics? Newly acquired data informs segmentation and targeting for advertising. Is there access to mobile device data that can be used for a new mobile coupon promotion? Can my CRM data be onboarded to anonymous IDs so I can reach the 80 percent of consumers who do not open my e-mail on Facebook?

- **Change management.** Not every employee and process survives a data transformation. Seek to memorialize the skills and personnel needed to achieve transformation based on the initial use cases you have selected in your go-to-market plan. Are there employees that are really good at running traditional database queries that can be trained on a new method of analytics? Is the way media performance is being reported going to be accepted and embraced by the analytics team?

You should be transparent about the changes that are going to take place, and you'll need to educate stakeholders on how their roles and responsibilities may change as new methods of measurement become available. Being cognizant of these five common pitfalls will help you drive the data transformation you require for success.

CASE IN POINT

Turner's Data Center of Excellence Puts Data at the Center and Drives Breakthrough Organizational Alignment

One sterling example of a company that progressed rapidly through all the stages of our capability maturity model was Turner, one of the wholly owned companies within Time Warner. Turner owns and operates some of the most important, premium media brands in the world, from niche television channels (Adult Swim), global news (CNN), and

sports (Turner Sports, Bleacher Report) to kids programming (Cartoon Network) and well-known cable offerings
such as Turner Classic Movies and TNT.

When we first started working with Turner, it faced
many of the challenges common to most major media companies: rapid fragmentation of its traditional audiences,
who were moving to digital channels and spending more
time on Facebook and other digital destinations, and
siloed internal data that made it difficult to sell its customers advertising packages spanning digital and traditional
channels. Stephano Kim, then EVP of digital strategy and
chief data strategist, was chartered by the CEO to solve
the problem. His strategy, in simple terms, was to increase
revenue from audience-based sales by leveraging people data to engage with Turner's audiences across web,
mobile, and over-the-top platforms. Given the diversity of
channels and outlets for Turner's content, it was a formi-
dable task, and certainly not for the meek of spirit. "We
knew we had diverse brands and compelling content as a
starting place, and we also knew that our audiences were
highly engaged with both," says Kim. "The issue was that,
as the industry shifted away from traditional media buying
metrics to more people-centric measurement, we needed
to prove that our audiences were highly valuable across
the entire multiplatform consumer journey."

The solution started with consolidating all of Turner's
first-party data across all consumer touchpoints and imple-

(continued)

menting a DMP, which Turner used to enrich its own data with second- and third-party sources to build high-value premium audiences. Kim oversaw this pioneering effort that quickly evolved into what is now known as the Turner Data Cloud, the repository for all of Turner's proprietary data assets. Kim's vision for the Turner Data Cloud was to leverage identity management capabilities and data feeds from the DMP, to ingest data from multiple sources and devices, and to stitch them into a single consumer ID that was connected to all Turner channels. Inside the Turner Data Cloud, Turner applied advanced analytics and data science to design custom audiences, model the overlap between linear cable and digital users, predict consumer behavior based on the propensity of consumers to engage with certain advertising brands, and assign lifetime value scores to virtually all its segments.

"The DMP was a fundamental first step on the way to unifying our audience data. It has become a central piece of our technology architecture in the Turner Data Cloud as a bridge to multiple consumer touch points. DMP was also a catalyst to get various teams to agree on the proper use and value of the data, identify skills and capabilities gaps to enable the data, and develop deeper insights from the data than we ever had before. We also needed the ongoing buy-in and support from leaders across sales, marketing, editorial, technology, and research, with the support of senior management. This is really just the starting point of a larger transformational journey for the company as we develop advanced use cases for content development and personalization, as well as more complex direct-to-consumer products."

Not content to rest on their laurels, today Kim and his team are extending the Turner Data Cloud so it's even more integrated into intelligent systems that support advanced ad sales products, multichannel marketing and content delivery, and financial modeling. Turner was the first major media company to embrace a center-of-excellence approach and achieve significant digital transformation years before its big media competitors understood the urgency. "We live in a very fast-moving environment where consumers have a growing set of options when it comes to content consumption. Our advertising clients are demanding richer solutions while the velocity of technological change increases daily," says Stephano. "We've tried to anchor our innovation and change management strategy around the right teams and operating models that puts both our consumers and data squarely at the center. This data- and consumer-centric model with agile execution provides us with a better chance of success."

CHAPTER 6

THE NEW BASIS OF COMPETITION: KNOW, PERSONALIZE, AND ENGAGE

We've argued that people data is fuel for modern marketing. Without techniques for capturing, extracting, organizing, and moving it, however, it is no better than tar trapped below the surface of the earth. Big data frameworks such as Spark, Kafka, and Dawn are the drilling, fracking, and pipelining techniques used to extract it. If, as we argued in Chapter 2, the traditional AIDA marketing funnel is dead, so, too, is the notion of traditional data warehousing systems, built to store data in rigid, structured environments. Gone, too, are the days when querying your people data asset required both specific sets of instructions and processing that unfolded in days. New data infrastructure gives us the ability to capture and make sense of data in minutes and seconds, at volumes and velocities that were simply unimaginable a decade ago.

In a technology context where pipe dreams become reality in a matter of quarters, it's critical for modern marketers to hone their sense not just regarding what's possible today, but also what's around the corner. As you work to develop a data-driven strategy for your own career and company, it would be foolish to assume that today's configuration of the pieces on the chessboard is the same one you'll face even just a year from now. Setting strategy against this backdrop requires anticipation of how the chess pieces are moving, and possibly even anticipation of a change in the underlying structure of the game. Standard chessboards today have eight rows and eight columns along the edges; what if that suddenly changed to eight by nine or nine by nine? Expert players would quickly modify their strategies to respond to the game's new layout. So, too, must the modern marketer.

THE THREE-LAYER MODEL

The new basis of competition for data-driven marketing follows a three-layer model, shown in Figure 6.1.

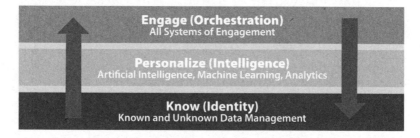

Figure 6.1 **A three-layer model—know, personalize, and engage—defines the future basis of competition for data-driven marketing.**

Know (the Who)

Data management forms the foundation upon which the other two layers rest. Its core purpose is to handle the "who." As described in Chapter 3, data management unifies and synchronizes data from multiple systems and sources (e-mail, commerce, online behavioral data, mobile, social, and other sources yet to be invented), so that marketers can see and engage with actual people, not faceless consumers or cookies. The future-proof version of this layer includes identity infrastructure, so that we know that the person watching the video online is the same person who bought the shoes. It should include facilities for executing each of the five big moves described in Chapter 4. Finally, it provides last-mile, intelligent connectivity to engage with users across any touchpoint. An example is making sure Dunkin's DD Perks members can be reached on Instagram when it's time to repost the ultimate Coolatta selfie from a hard-core fan, or suppressing the e-mail discount offer on a new product for the customer who is irritated and currently working with your service department to fix the product he already bought.

Many marketers have developed an intimate understanding of the who from persona-building exercises and CRM systems. Procter & Gamble could have bought several small countries with the money it has allocated over the years to build perfect demographic and psychographic personas to understand various "moments of truth." Such insights help companies get to the bottom of why certain people are more likely to grab Bounty paper towels off the shelf rather than Brawny. But the who has now shattered into dozens of distinct subsegments and millions of user identities across dozens of addressable platforms. There are no silver bullets or magic beans. Selling Bounty in this new context entails a strategic commitment to people data and meaningful investment in data management so that P&G can continually find Bounty intenders and keep Bounty loyalists from drifting to another brand.

Personalize (the What)

Next comes the artificial intelligence layer, which helps marketers make sense of all the signals in their people data so they can delight their customers with exactly the right next move. Think of this layer as the "what." Based on the attributes of this customer segment, what creative message should we send a customer? Based on this customer's recent activity and profile, should we put him into an e-mail "nurture" campaign and attempt to influence him over time; send him an e-mail offer because he looks like he might be interested in a particular product; or phone him right now, give the salesperson a flashing "call now" prompt in her CRM system, and nudge her to close the deal? Artificial intelligence systems peer into vast troves of granular data and use machine learning and data science to parse patterns in people behavior to recommend the next best action.

Marketers are also leaning in heavily on the what, hiring data scientists to crunch data to drive better decisions about how to engage customers. They are feverishly building propensity models based on website activity, licensing attribution technology to get a better sense of which marketing channel should get the most credit for delivering a sale, and churning through past years' data to build "lifetime value" scores that can help them decide which customers are worth more than others. This knowledge is all but useless unless they nail the problem of identity and put this decision-making information into the systems that can activate it. Without the knowledge that the person who just visited my website leases a brand-new car every three years and prefers a two-door sedan, all of the smartest user scoring and propensity modeling is idle theory and mathematical model building in search of a purpose. We identify the who and what layers separately because the problems they pose are distinct, but they are, in this way, inextricably linked.

In the late 1990s and 2000s, the mathematical model building required to answer these what-related questions was divorced from execution and usually unfolded after the fact via attribution and media mix modeling efforts. Thankfully, in recent years execution and analysis have been brought closer and closer together. The best way to think about their dynamic is as the interlocking of a big gear (the attribution or mix modeling algorithm) with a smaller gear (a fast-twitch piece of code that does something interesting in a user's browser or device). Attribution and mix modeling algorithms are computed offline in batch mode, usually according to a weekly cadence, and work by updating slow-changing parameters of an underlying mathematical model. Online algorithms combine the results of the offline algorithms with the actions of a specific user to personalize the user's experience in real time, making a run-time decision to show a red car instead of a gray car on the next page that a particular user sees, as Peugeot does with dynamic content personalization.

Without this binding together of analytics and execution, the most powerful AI is like Stephen Hawking (may he rest in peace) without his translation machine, a genius who cannot actualize his ideas in the world. In this way, sensing, engaging, and sense making increasingly unfold in real time together. In the near future they will be tightly bound together via a capability we call pipelining, which we will discuss in the next chapter.

AI practitioners, like any new technology priesthood, use jargon ("multilayer neural networks," "mixed Gaussian association models," etc.) to dazzle and confuse others and to perpetuate their belief that they're too smart to be questioned. As a practitioner, your objective shouldn't be to become buzzword-compliant, but rather to relentlessly focus your teams on the practical benefits of these new techniques and technologies. AI can solve a lot of adorable but inconsequential problems. Pointing it at the biggest, most consequential ones is the fastest path to a meaningful payoff for your company—and a promotion for yourself.

Engage (the When and Where)

On the top is a layer that's frequently overlooked but increasingly important. It is the orchestration layer, which coordinates critical "when" and "where" decisions. When should I send that "$500 bonus for taking a test drive" offer or the "close this deal now" signal inside a salesperson's CRM system? Should I send the e-mail offer before or after my target has watched an online video? If we acknowledge that competitive modern marketing requires perfect understanding of the customer journey and precise knowledge of when and where to send the right message, then you can run, but you can't hide from the fundamental challenge of orchestration.

Orchestration requires a deep understanding of the power of *sequences* and *combinations*. Actionable intelligence about combinations, for example, could reveal that a portfolio of touchpoints that includes e-mail, video, social, and display is 27 percent more likely to result in a conversion than a portfolio of just e-mail, social, and display. Video can, in this example, exert a measurable benefit when applied in conjunction with other channels and touchpoints.

Adroit marketers are beginning to leverage these portfolio effects with exciting results, particularly in light of the uneven, inefficient pricing that plagues the digital media landscape. Given the channel control exerted by a few oligopolists in social media, inventory is frequently priced to the breaking point, while under-leveraged channels such as direct mail can offer, perhaps surprisingly, much higher value for money. Just as financiers look to include underpriced asset classes with higher expected returns in their portfolio, savvy marketers are increasingly looking to optimize the total effect of their marketing spend across a bundle of channels and touchpoints, not just a single channel or the last touchpoint, as too many attribution and media mix models implicitly require.

When a boy is courting a girl, he quickly learns that an invitation to lunch followed by dinner followed by flowers spurs more affection, and less fear, than showing up on day one with a large bouquet of red roses and a marriage proposal. So it is for a marketer engaging with prospects. Our experience has taught us that the *sequence* in which customers receive your messages, respectfully and artfully delivered, can dramatically change their propensity to engage and respond.

By looking at the time-stamped sequence of delivered messages, a marketer may be able to determine that inexpensive display advertising works to increase engagement on more expensive video impressions. If you knew that preceding a $25 CPM video ad with $2 CPM banner impressions meant an increase of 20 percent in completed video views for a particular campaign, and also knew that completed video views increased the propensity to purchase by 10 percent, then it's safe to say you would always sequence those messages so that display preceded video.

The grand unification of the who, what, when, and where—the pinnacle of orchestration—is what we call the consumer journey. It's not futurism or idle abstraction. It is, rather, an actionable construct that pioneering marketers are using to drive deeper, more effective consumer engagement today.

THE CONSUMER JOURNEY

In Chapter 3 we talked about "data in" and "data out." And in Chapter 4, we discussed "data back in," explaining that it refers to all the data from addressable interactions that we can capture and time-stamp. When was the display ad clicked on? What creative was viewed? What part of my website did a user interact with? When did a user respond to an SMS push notification? In isolation, each of these events is almost useless. When stitched together in a sequence, however, they paint a powerful picture of the journey that consumers take on their way to an outcome that matters for the marketer: a download, a test drive, a click, an e-mail response, a purchase.

Journeys take hundreds of millions of interactions. Visualize them in an *ordered sequence*—not just a combination—to get a sense of how consumers engaged from first brand exposure, all the way through to a specific event, such as a site visit or e-commerce purchase. A typical journey analysis requires the distillation of patterns across thousands of different variables. Figure 6.2 shows an example. One particular digital campaign we analyzed for a television broadcaster featured 601 different placements, 144 ads, dozens of different creative executions, 33 different campaigns, and dozens of audience segments targeted across thousands of websites. Once you do the math, you come to grips quickly with the combinatorial complexity: literally millions of combinations can occur in a single campaign.

Source Manifest

Activity Source	Property Type	Properties
ad_impression	placement	601
	ad	144
	creative	144
	campaign	33
	channel	1
click	placement	411
	ad	141
	campaign	28
	channel	1
event	event	16
pixel	site	26

Segment Manifest

Segment Name	Converters	Journeys
A&E_BatesMotel_(DFP)	0	27,045
A&E_BatesMotel[3rd]_(DFP)	1,686	802,210
A+E_BatesMotel[A+E]Suppressed_(DFP)	332	75,573
A+E_BatesMotel[WB]_(DFP)	332	75,573
A+E_BatesMotel[WB][A+E]_(DFP)	332	75,573
A+E_BatesMotelOnly_[WB]_1x90	51	9,096
A+E_BatesMotelOnly-Overlap[WB][A+E]_(D..	0	34
A+E_BatesMotelOnly[A+E]Suppressed_(DF..	125	23,340
A+E_BatesMotelOnly[WB]_(DFP)	125	23,340
A+E_BatesMotelOnly[WB][A+E]_(DFP)	125	23,340
A+E_BatesMotelOverlap[WB][A+E]_(DFP)	1	130
A+E_UnRealAffinity_[A+E]	37	13,583
A+E_UnRealShowlist_[A+E]	131	86,104
AccountType_Anonymous_[FLX]_2	1,686	557,816
AccountType_Authenticated_[FLX]_2	308	61,621

Figure 6.2 **This report shows all the variables involved in analyzing the customer journey: dozens of segments, hundreds of ad placements, multiple creatives, and more.**

With the ability to view the delivery of ads in sequence, we can determine that inexpensive display ads were not effective on their own, but they helped drive an increase in the completion of video views where consumers watched an entire 30-second ad. We also might understand that consumers who completed a video ad view were likely to convert. As above, knowing that relatively cheap display advertising drives increases in video ad completion, which in turn drives more sales, offers just a single example of the portfolio effects of sequences and combinations.

Figure 6.3 shows a stack-ranked set of journey sequences that lead to measurable conversion lift. Understanding these can help marketers activate specific journeys and manage the delivery of different interactions across systems of engagement such as e-mail, SMS, display, video, and mobile advertising. Because they are not limited to just media, marketers can use journeys to also understand how certain "real-life" touchpoints, such as an interaction with a call center or comment on a community website, shaped the consumer's overall brand engagement or product purchase.

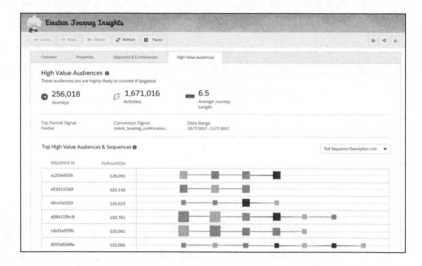

Figure 6.3 **This journey insights report for a popular travel site shows 256,018 journeys containing over 1.6 million individual activities. The average journey had over six touchpoints before conversion.**

Subaru Australia's Journey Analysis Results in More Test Drives

When Subaru's Australian division started to analyze its consumer journey data, it became apparent that a particular series of touchpoints always resulted in more lift, a higher propensity to fill out the "request a test drive" form on its website. Customers who committed to taking a test drive were highly likely to go to the dealership, hop in the car, and ultimately take it off the lot. The consumer's journey spans many months and multiple touchpoints, all key moments when a potential buyer gets closer to or farther away from brand consideration.

Simply by analyzing the journey that web visitors took, page by page, to the "request a test drive" form, Subaru started to understand the ideal journey. By optimizing or eliminating key points that created "fall-off" in the journey, Subaru was able to increase form fill-outs by 10 percent. Ten percent more people in the dealership every single month is a seismic uptick, particularly when considering the average revenue per vehicle sold. Having access to time-based data and a granular understanding of individual journeys based on buyer type made all the difference.

Using journeys, sophisticated marketers are moving beyond happy coincidences ("Wow, who knew that showing them a video before we hit them with the e-mail solicitation could have such a huge effect!") to the design of customer journeys that reliably generate the results they're after. For all the channels and touchpoints available, there are literally billions of possible sequences, as Figure 6.4 shows. Identifying the top 10 that actually work is a sophisticated exercise in combinatorial mathematics.

(continued)

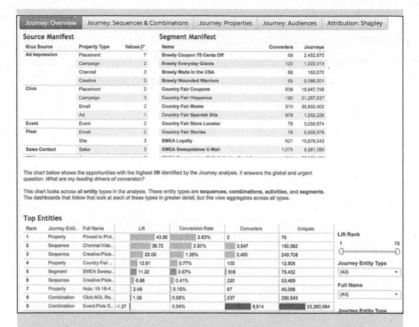

Figure 6.4 **A source manifest for a typical journey insights report***
*Campaigns can feature hundreds of millions of activities, or data inputs, and tens of millions of journeys, or the sequence of events between an initial encounter with a brand and a purchase, for example. Only machine learning can quickly surface insights from such large data sets.

GETTING ELEPHANTS TO DANCE

Orchestrating an effective consumer journey also entails getting elephants to dance. Suppose you are an airline marketer and your data management system identifies Miami-to-New York travelers and you're targeting the segment to get butts in seats for flights with excess capacity. If the buying system that your agency or marketer teams rely on to buy advertising (a demand-side platform) takes a week or even a day to receive and act on a signal sent from the center of the "TIE fighter" from Chapter 3, the flight you're try-ing to fill could depart before your media systems start messag-ing Miami-to-New York travelers, a bizarre but not uncommon scenario. This dynamic is in effect across every modality: mobile, social, video, gaming, and display advertising.

We call this the "Can you catch what I'm pitching?" principle, and it's a useful question to bring to your discussions with external technology vendors and internal IT teams. If a last-mile execution system can't catch what your first-party data management sys-tem is pitching, your best-laid strategies for multichannel orches-tration come to nothing. The good news is that integration across all these systems has settled into a well-established pattern, and most of the technical teams across all the major vendors know how to execute the required handshakes. Practitioners are wise, though, to take note of the general challenge and push their part-ners to resolve it quickly.

PUTTING IT ALL TOGETHER

While today's marketers don't need to be experts at every layer of the stack, they need a practical understanding of the possible effects and benefits. Marketers might excel at generating ana-lytics results with the world's best AI, but such results only sat-isfy curiosity if they're divorced from media execution. Marketers can string together the perfect cross-channel execution system to make e-mail, mobile, and display experiences work together, but these marketers will fail to engage the right users because they lack the data management required to identify customers across devices. They might be able to execute sequences and combina-tions tied to arbitrary triggers, but without AI to tell them what to send to whom and when, their orchestration engine is a beautiful dancer with strength and flexibility but no moves.

In sum, without AI or orchestration, data management is a massive data store with elaborate plumbing and piping, bereft of insight and coordination. Data management without AI easily devolves into sending the wrong signal faster. Without orchestration, it occasionally gets lucky and sends a relevant signal, but at the wrong time. Properly synchronized and woven together, data management, orchestration, and AI form the backbone of any future-proof marketing engine.

Large software companies such as Salesforce, Oracle, and Adobe are putting this layer cake of capabilities together to build marketing clouds toward the objective of offering a one-stop shop for the CMO. As consumers shift their attention to digital experiences, marketers need to be techier than ever before, which has led to an explosion of chief data officers, chief experience officers, and chief digital officers. Much of their work has been dedicated to leveraging different technologies to transform marketing objectives into tangible results. It began with licensing orchestration systems such as ad servers, e-mail platforms, and social media tools; evolved to the data management layer to unify people identity and connect the pipes they built; and currently hinges on the application of artificial intelligence for further competitive advantage.

CHAPTER 7

SEVEN FORECASTS
TO LIGHT UP YOUR
FUTURE SENSORS

In the future, we will enjoy personal supersonic travel at everyday low prices, solve all genetic defects through personalized gene therapy, and store and project our consciousness digitally after we die. We don't claim to know *when* all those things will happen. We merely posit that they *will*.

See how easy that was? The farther out you go, the more feasible and fun predicting the future becomes.

Things get tougher when you come closer to the present. First, it's easy to mistake clarity for proximity. Digital marketing offers an object lesson in this regard. In 1999, Peters and Rodgers established 1:1 marketing as a "but of course" imperative for the early 2000s. The idea resonated, but it wasn't feasible. Computing whether a consumer belonged to a segment of mayonnaise lovers from Wisconsin shopping for a family of at least four people was, using relational database technology at the time, a job that took 8 to 12 hours to complete. We know because we were there. We tried it and we failed. Over 15 years later, we're computing the mayonnaise segment in minutes, moving quickly to seconds. But targeting this single ad or offer to *just you* in real time, which is the premise of 1:1 marketing, mostly eludes us still.

The second fly in the ointment is wild cards. They are frequent sources of delight and surprise, and they can overtake us suddenly. When I (Tom) first encountered a camera on my Motorola Razor phone 15 years ago, I thought it was the stupidest, most useless thing I'd ever seen. Why take a grainy picture on a phone when you already own a perfectly awesome digital camera? In the annals of wrongology, my questioning the near-term inevitability of the mobile phone puts me in the unenviable company of Christian end-time zealots and climate change deniers. Like many, I quickly had to revamp my assumptions and acclimate to the new normal. Wild cards upend prior assumptions and scramble what you thought you liked, what you thought you knew, and where we're all headed.

Despite the hazards, we think we'd be remiss if we didn't offer a perspective on where data-driven marketing is headed in the next few years. Our goal is not to be prescient or perfect. (We're reminded of Prince Humperdinck from *The Princess Bride* who frequently began his officious pronouncements with, "Unless I'm wrong—and I'm *never* wrong. . . .") Our ambition is to sketch what our friend Paul Saffo calls the "cone of uncertainty,"[1] which begins from the present and fans out in a disciplined way to establish the perimeter of what's possible and therefore credible. By stimulating and conditioning your "future sensors" in this way, we hope to sensitize you to surprise, help you anticipate what could be around the corner, and suggest useful questions to help manage the hype-to-reality ratio from vendors and partners. We might even provoke you to disprove our projections—or if we're lucky, to make them so.

The best way to predict the future, after all, is to build it.

1. ARTIFICIAL INTELLIGENCE REDUCES SCUT WORK AND MAKES MARKETING MORE STRATEGIC

When you multiply two positive quantities together and they equal the same constant K, it's called an inversely proportional relationship. One of the quantities goes up while the other necessarily goes down. An example is Boyle's law, $PV = K$, which describes the inversely proportional relationship between a gas's pressure and its volume. If you have steam in a container, Boyle's law tells us that the pressure it exerts will be low if the container is large. This makes sense; more space gives steam molecules more room to roam. Conversely, if you shrink the container, you decrease the volume that the steam is allowed to occupy, thereby increasing its pressure.

A similar interplay is at work between systems based on workflow and systems based on AI. Call it "Salesforce's law of workflow":

$$\text{Artificial intelligence} \times \text{workflow} = K$$

Put simply, as the IQ of the technology you use to run your business increases, time and resources devoted to workflow decrease proportionately. AI, when given more space to roam, naturally reduces the need for workflow.

At a conceptual level, AI-enabled experiences by their very design reduce time spent reacting, logging, and recording. They open up more opportunity for doing, thinking, solving, closing, supporting, and negotiating. With AI, your people are naturally connected to the dynamics that drive real value for your business. Even better, they're unshackled to attack them with a mobile phone as the only tether to the mother ship they really need.

When you can anticipate what's around the corner, seize opportunities, and prevent problems before they have a chance to manifest, you're spending less time fire-fighting and diving for catches. When your tools are surfacing possibilities and recommending the next right action, there's less need for you to annotate every move you make in a ledger or software system. In an AI-enabled business, employees are out there selling, servicing, and supporting customers, not checking statuses and logging actions like bureaucrats in a Soviet-era commune. With help from AI, employees can respond gracefully to surprise, which in turn dampens the need for policies and procedures and the value of tools whose sole purpose is to enforce adherence to predefined processes.

Let's consider an example from conventional CRM. In the old world, salespeople were fed leads, pursued them, winnowed them into a smaller set of promising sales cycles, and came back to their CRM system to record the fact that the prospect had moved, for example, from a "verbal yes" to "in contract." Modern AI-enabled systems don't just record; they recommend. In the new world, AI suggests leads to pursue and tactics to help move a prospect from curious to serious based on the behavior and buyer attributes of customers in similar geographies or market sectors. The systems update themselves to reflect the progress of a sales cycle without the clutter of hearsay and anecdote, and reduce the inherent motivational bias of the salesperson to convey a shinier state of affairs than might actually be the case. They can also eliminate bias in the opposite direction, where a hyperconservative sales rep (the "sandbagger") understates the likelihood of closing a customer.

The inverse relationship between workflow and AI is especially acute in the realm of modern marketing. While the abundance of data tied to consumer engagement certainly makes marketing more data driven, that doesn't mean that marketers will be glued to their screens like Wall Street quants searching for numerical patterns. Through AI, marketers become more empowered with insights about what customers need, what they like, what they hate, where they're still trying to make up their minds. This, in turn, drives more cognitive work—building a new theory of the consumer, rapidly testing new engagement methods, launching new channels—and shifts the balance of a marketer's work. In the new world, marketers are still interacting with software, but the ratio of time spent on scut work to time spent on strategy is dramatically and forever altered.

As with conventional CRM, logging and coordinating the steps of an advertising campaign is not the best use of a marketer's time. Leave that to the machines. As data-driven methods continue to take root and flourish, modern marketers can expect to see the following changes in their day-to-day jobs:

- Instead of specifying targeting criteria, flighting details, and creatives, marketers specify campaign goal engagement metrics like desired number of conversions, desired number of sales and, in general, desired number of outcomes.

- With end-to-end tracking, measurement, and brand effectiveness strategies in place, marketers finally have a way to measure the impact of a brand-awareness campaign.

- Media optimization across channels finally becomes a fully machine-driven experience. The art of reaching the right audience at the right time at the right price to achieve the right outcome becomes the norm, finally moving out of the black magic, voodoo-like state it occupies today.

2. DATA PIPELINING BECOMES A DURABLE DIFFERENTIATOR

About two years ago, Google, arguably the most advanced AI company on the planet, put the algorithm it uses for much of its machine learning, called TensorFlow, into the public domain. By open-sourcing TensorFlow, Google effectively gave its crown jewels to the entire world. Why would it do that? One argument could be that, by open-sourcing TensorFlow, Google can enroll a much larger collection of the world's brains into making it better. But TensorFlow was already fire-tested and extremely well developed before Google made its decision, and Google is hardly a philanthropy or nonprofit. Open-sourcing TensorFlow was evidence of a deeper, more strategic understanding: *the algorithms don't matter nearly as much as the data that feeds them.* And Google, from our vantage point, is sitting on the world's largest, most valuable store of data.

As algorithms like TensorFlow and many other AI techniques reach their maturity points, nonspecialists can deploy them quickly via well-documented interfaces and widely available toolsets. There are many companies in Silicon Valley, for example, founded by hard-charging, self-taught techies who didn't graduate from college and never took an advanced math class. Nevertheless, they are successfully developing sophisticated AI systems in a variety of problem areas—applying sensor data to detect product breakdowns before they occur, for example, or parsing massive user-generated feeds in search of hate speech or fake news. They're able to achieve these breakthroughs because the tools are simple to use and the underlying algorithms are consistent and stable. AI's ascendance is thus marked by an interesting irony: the people who are most expertly deploying it are not AI experts.

Accordingly, companies that attempt to win in the new data-driven sphere by hiring machine learning experts and developing their own AI from scratch are headed for heartbreak. There's no way they can out-Google Google, which has already broadcast that even *it* doesn't ascribe proprietary value to its AI. As every company amasses more data and applies increasingly fungible AI to crunch it, isolating sources of future competitive advantage gets tricky.

Let's imagine a horse race between two companies operating from roughly comparable stores of data competing in the same consumer-facing sector—CPG, travel, or entertainment, say. How do we predict which company will win the battle for consumer engagement? We believe that the winner is the company that achieves something geeky but fundamental in the infrastructure it uses to capture and connect consumer data. We call it "pipe-lining": the ability to synchronize data vertically up and down the three-layer model in a manner that ensures access to, and activation of, data that is:

- Elastic

- Self-healing

- Available

- "Correct enough"

- Monitorable

- Secure

- Clean

Let's unpack each of these so that you can have the right conversation with your marketing cloud vendor or internal IT partner.

Elasticity means that as your data sets grow, you can add hardware and software to manage them so that they operate as a single logical entity. There are no silos, ponds, or backwaters; the data sets function as a single, enormous lake. Rather than adding more memory or storage to a single huge machine, elasticity gives you the ability to add multiple machines on the fly in a plug-and-play fashion. A large new data set from a partner or a new marketing campaign suddenly arrives? No need to wait two months for hardware to arrive and your IT organization to install and configure new databases; elasticity allows you to ingest and integrate it right away.

Elasticity is the precondition for self-healing and availability. If one of your pieces of hardware (what techies call a "node") crashes, the others pick up the pieces and the overall system absorbs the shock gracefully. As long as you're willing to feed the pipeline with new hardware, your system remains online and always available. This is not to be taken for granted: it represents a significant change from older methods where IT administrators took large systems offline for many hours or days at a time for maintenance, tuning, and reconfiguration.

There are two aspects to availability: when and where. A highly available data pipeline ensures that you get access to data and results at the velocity required to make timely business decisions. When you ask, "How many moms in Minnesota bought cream cheese from December through February?" a high-availability pipeline enables an answer in seconds or minutes—not a day or a week later or in a monthly marketing snapshot. The "where" aspect of availability requires that data be stored in different forms and at different granularities in multiple locations, including browsers and devices, to be activated whenever the data is needed. In this sense, pipelining underpins the concept of a data fabric, evoked in Chapter 1 and worthy of our full attention now. Like a vast quilt, a data fabric covers the broadest possible array of devices, uses, and touchpoints, all of it powered by interconnected pipelines functioning quietly in the background.

A big aha moment at Krux was when we recognized that the availability of *some* data for real-time decision making was much better than its complete absence. In other words, *availability* of data trumps *consistency* of data. As distributed data storage systems have become more pervasive, services that operate on top of such systems have evolved to embrace the notion of *eventual consistency*. IT groups trained in old-school methods frequently get stuck on this point: they won't release data unless they're 100 percent certain that all of it is in place and is 100 percent consistent. In a commerce system, products ordered by a single user, for example, won't always match the products in delivery to that same user. If you seek to know how many products he or she bought, you might get inconsistent answers depending on when you query the system. Odds are high that you prefer some information, particularly when it reflects a fast-moving phenomenon like a customer order, to zero information. Pipelining allows you to maintain always-on access to data, with confidence that if it's not perfectly consistent in the moment you request it, it will soon get there. In this sense, a properly architected pipeline ensures that perfectly correct data never stands in the way of the availability of data that is correct enough.

Pipelines are self-monitoring. The location, granularity, and sources of data flowing through them can be readily inspected at any moment. They know if they're broken, and they are instrumented to self-report their status with messages such as "ETL broke, fixing it now" and "Data got corrupted at one of the sources, re-ingesting now" (Figure 7.1).

Monthly Users by ID Type		
Id Type	User Count ⇌	% of Total
KUID_COOKIE	3,511,472,553	88.07%
SAFARI	378,476,620	9.49%
IOS_IDFA	35,993,893	0.90%
CLIENT_FIRST_PARTY_ID	29,449,517	0.74%
ANDROID_IDFA	21,489,871	0.54%
OTHER	10,358,869	0.26%
Grand Total	3,987,241,323	100.00%

Figure 7.1 **Data pipelining is fundamental to modern business. The famous Twitter Fail Whale (left) and Microsoft's infamous blue screen of death were moments when consumers realized the complexity of the software and data pipelining running in the background.**

In 2010 we believed that third-party data was on a path to commoditization and that first-party data would surge in value to marketers and publishers. From our vantage point this has largely come to pass. As we have outlined along the way, organizations are increasingly moving toward second-party data-sharing relationships that allow them to share data with select partners on terms and timing of their choosing. If Ticketmaster/LiveNation decides to make data available to Heineken in a peer-to-peer fashion, Ticketmaster/LiveNation needs confidence that, once the usage period is over, the data it shared still belongs to it, is no longer available to Heineken, and hasn't leaked into any of Heineken's systems or Heineken's partners' systems. A dumb pipe can't deliver these assurances. A smarter pipeline executes logic to (*a*) comply with evolving data privacy regulations and standards and (*b*) enforce ownership as data within a pipeline is transformed and propagated across partners. With policy-managed pipelining, you no longer send massive data files containing valuable information about all your users; instead, you can share a narrower subset of users in predefined segments, with terms and pricing established and enforced via what we call a "restricted data lease."

The highest power of pipelines is realized via what we call "chaining," the mechanism by which multiple pipelines are merged to construct larger pipelines. Because each pipeline has built-in controls for provenance and compliance, all chains built from individual pipelines automatically inherit the provenance and compliance controls of their constituent parts. Pipelining architected in this fashion gives you confidence that none of the data you're using to run the business infringes on privacy or poses sourcing risk because every stage of the pipeline is secure. Every upstream pipeline releases only authorized, contractually clean data into the pipeline.

Without effective pipelining, orchestration is virtually inoperable, because you're unable to refresh the data you're using to target users at every step of their journey as quickly as they're zigging and zagging from surface to surface. If your pipeline takes a day to refresh, then the velocity of every orchestration step can't be any faster than a day. This means that you won't see users who are moving from e-mail in the morning to video later in the afternoon. *Latency mismatches* like this are what blow up most orchestration efforts while they're still on the launch pad. Put simply, you can't orchestrate what you can't see. Fast, flexible pipelining is the solution, and will undoubtedly power successful orchestration at Layer 2 for years to come.

3. CONSUMER IoT ENCIRCLES CRM

We've observed that the devices and gizmos we interact with almost every minute of every day are throwing off precious data regarding what we like and what we hate. This universe of gadgets, referred to as the Internet of Things (IoT), constitutes a new data fabric that covers practically every nook and cranny of our daily lives. As we've argued, data-driven companies seeking to interact with consumers understand that, to earn our trust and our attention, they need to engage with us across that entire fabric—not just laptops and mobile phones, but music players, televisions, health monitors, thermostats, refrigerators, and even coffee makers. There's no one device or channel they can rely on to understand what we want. Rather they face a symphony of touchpoints, collectively known as the consumer IoT.

A CRM stalwart might hear this and say, "That's fine. Just fly all that data in to my CRM system, and I'll use it for selling and servicing customers." But legacy CRM isn't architected to handle the volume and velocity of data from consumer IoT, and consumer IoT isn't just a new source of data. It's a new data fabric, and it requires an entirely new foundation for capturing, analyzing, segmenting, and activating data, known today as DMP. Next-generation data management systems built on new technologies (as opposed to late-twentieth-century ones) naturally handle the volume and velocity of data thrown off by consumer IoT. Best-ofbreed providers are already working to re-architect existing CRM footprints to make them IoT-ready via next-gen DMP.

The difference between CRM and consumer IoT goes beyond sources and uses of data. Our mantra has been that handhelds don't buy beer or travel packages; people do. But here's the rub: these pesky devices, when stitched together in this new fabric, *know* quite a lot about us. Decades ago when CRM was first hatched, we registered our interest in a vacation travel package by driving to a travel agency and talking to an agent. It was a hand-raising, highly intentional act. Today, by employing the data management techniques we've explored in this book, airlines, hotel chains, and online travel aggregators capture data from the many devices you use to infer your interest in a vacation travel package, whether you're explicitly aware of it or not.

If your company seeks to catalyze and manage customer relationships in the new regime, your journey *necessarily* takes you from recording the hand-raising acts of your customers in a legacy CRM system to intelligently deducing their needs across consumer IoT. Primarily for this reason, we believe that consumer IoT as a category will soon encircle and upend conventional CRM.

Will consumer IoT supplant conventional CRM through revolution or evolution? As these things usually go, we can likely expect to see a Darwinian melee wherein a few incumbents die violently, a few established players successfully cross over, and one or two new contenders emerge from the soup. What this entails for the practitioner considering the technology alternatives ahead is deeper attention to questions of scale, volume, velocity, and variety of data. You'll need to probe deeply with your tech teams and vendors to answer these questions:

- How many petabytes of data can the new CRM ingest without falling over? What APIs does the CRM provide for ingesting different types of data? Ingesting petabytes at scale requires APIs and pipelines that operate in batch mode. Does the CRM provide real-time and batch modes for data ingestion in a way that's easily accessible to the marketer?

- How much data is *truly* available for analysis and real-time activation?

- Does the CRM system impose any restrictions on the type of data being ingested? Does it provide "schema-on-read" semantics and offer flexibility in data ingestion so that the data schema can be applied at "query time" as opposed to "load and ingest time"? (Schema-on-read systems store data first and then apply a taxonomy when the data is queried, as opposed to schema-on-write systems that require the taxonomy to be prebuilt. The latter type of design limits queries to a rigid structure, making it difficult to find interesting, new insights from data.)

- What infrastructure for identity resolution is at work across different customer-facing systems? Recognizing that it's you in a commerce system that supports your purchase but not recognizing that it's the same you inside a service system designed to help you after your purchase is the path to perdition. An extensible identity infrastructure that supports a generalized set of identity keys—including but not limited to devices (cookies, MAIDs, OTT, etc.), e-mails (plain text and hashed), cohorts, and households—is increasingly becoming a table-stakes requirement for modern CRM systems. Does the new CRM system provide such an identity infrastructure and accompanying set of services?

• Given that we are moving toward a world where my coffee machine knows more about the type of coffee that I drink than I do, does the CRM seamlessly integrate with devices, APIs, and other services that are increasingly going to become stewards of consumer data?

At first glance the abundance of devices appears more like a dog's breakfast than a single fabric; we should wonder how it hangs together. Through what central control point or gateway could consumer IoT swallow conventional CRM? To answer this question, we need to consider the story of Sonos, a successful provider of Internet-connected music systems.

> **CASE IN POINT**
>
> **Sonos Embraces the De Facto Gateway for Consumer IoT**
>
> Ten years ago, Sonos offered not just Wi-Fi-enabled systems that allow you to play music in different zones across your house, but also proprietary controllers to curate and select the music you want to play from Internet music services such as Pandora and Spotify and personal music libraries on iTunes or other platforms. When you bought
>
> *(continued)*

a Sonos system, you paid for both the player and the controller. In a prescient move well ahead of its time, Sonos decided to sunset its controller as a separate device and migrate it fully and exclusively to a mobile app. With the benefit of hindsight, it's easy to look at this today as a no-regrets decision, but Sonos made the move at a time when mobile apps were barely nascent. By attaching the controller to a device that consumers conveniently already kept in their pockets, the company made it easy to initiate and conduct listening experiences. This, in turn, increased revenue and usage for Sonos, despite the short-term hit from foregone sales of the controller.

The Sonos lesson carries with it a central implication for consumer IoT and CRM. Our handhelds have become not just all-in-one phones, cameras, and music players, but the remote control we use to manage our daily lives. The controller for consumer IoT is your handheld; iOS and Android apps are its buttons. From today's perch it's difficult to see how the stable equilibrium that has emerged among Apple, Google, and hundreds of consumer-facing brands such as Amazon, Uber, and Spotify could be suddenly upended. For the foreseeable future, Apple iOS and Google Android will serve as the central gateway for consumer IoT.

4. CONTENT MANAGEMENT GETS BLOWN UP, PUT BACK TOGETHER, AND CLOUDIFIED

Marketers aim to dazzle consumers and bring them closer to their brands with cooler content. Digital experiences generate data. The consumption of content and media is itself a valuable source of data for the modern marketer. For this reason it's critical to factor content explicitly into our view of the future.

Today, the software that marketers use to deliver content experiences in desktop and mobile environments is known as content management systems (CMSs). In the early years of the industrial Internet, writing HTML from scratch for every new web page that a company wanted to publish was laborious, and hiring an army of web designers and website managers to handle the corresponding complexity wasn't sustainable or smart. Technology providers such as Vignette[2] understood that corporations needed help managing their web content. A system for storing and managing web content and pushing it out across corporate websites, which were becoming increasingly complex and multilayered, was urgently required. A CMS filled that need.

Markets are efficient, and in the case of CMSs, they were hyperefficient. As more and more corporations flocked to the web, a flurry of CMS providers emerged to automate the creation and maintenance of corporate websites. While companies like Salesforce were pioneering the pay-as-you-go model for software as a service (SaaS), CMSs missed the business model transition altogether and continued peddling packaged software, delivered and installed mostly on premise. As a result of competition, CMS prices were reduced to levels that hollowed out most stand-alone CMS providers, and CMS as a software category became undifferentiated and cheap.

Fast-forward to today. Most companies are operating a mix of home-grown systems stitched together with occasional components from a few external providers to handle their CMS needs. They're beginning to recognize, however, that the cacophony of the home-grown CMS carries its own hazards and inefficiencies. Increasingly, they're crying out for a standard SaaS solution—perhaps without all the bells and whistles they've concocted, but they'll trade those off for lower maintenance costs and a steadier, more reliable upgrade path.

It's a peculiar fact that there are currently no software alternatives to fill the void. Subscribing as we do to the efficiency of markets, however, we believe the imbalance is entering the early stage of a correction:

- The next-generation CMS will be brought to market first as a subscription service.

- It will be provisioned, managed, and delivered from the cloud, not as on-premise software.

- Like a DMP, which recognizes no useful distinction between a handheld DMP versus a desktop DMP versus a tablet DMP versus a set-top DMP, it will be cross-device capable.

- Future CMSs will evolve from rule-based execution that delivers static media assets to data-driven, AI-enabled execution that dynamically deploys content for always-on consumer engagement. Real-time personalization won't be an add-on or a separate module; it will be a core capability woven into the CMS's basic function.

- And the hardest part of all, next-gen CMS will support dynamic content across multiple modalities: HTML and all its future incarnations, video, virtual reality, etc. All of it.

For the practitioner, the key questions to consider in examining future CMS alternatives are:

- How many channels, surfaces, and media types does it support?

- Is it true SaaS, offering a meaningful upgrade path?

- Does it include native facilities for real-time personalization tasks such as A/B testing?

- Does it include native facilities for seamless integration with traditional publisher-focused capabilities such as revenue and yield management and user experience management?

5. THE ALL-IN-ONE INTELLIGENT MARKETING HUB EMERGES

There was a time when conventional CRM, operating on gigabytes of data via batch-oriented processing, was sufficient: when customers purchased goods in a store after seeing an advertisement on TV, when they possessed the tiniest fraction of the touchpoints and screens they now use to express their preferences and propensities, when their purchases moved through supply chains that fulfilled orders in weeks and months. That was before the consumer web, same-day delivery, and multichannel marketing spoiled us all. Whether it comes to buying, selling, browsing, analyzing, fixing, healing, or building, we want it to be personal. We want it perfect. And we want it *now*.

We believe a new kind of B2C engine—we call it the intelligent marketing hub (IMH)—will soon make *every* interaction with a consumer personal, perfect, and now. E-mail systems or video or ad servers won't perform this kind of personalization in individual silos that hardly talk to each other. IMH will coordinate all of it from an aerial command point. Think of it as the grand realization of the three-layer model.

IMH will essentially act as a brain and a nervous system for transmitting directions to any external system responsible for rendering a piece of content to an individual consumer. This includes digital content, social, mobile, video, gaming, virtual reality, etc. It works by tagging every experience a company might want to put in front of a user—an ad, a video, an offer, a text message—with a piece of code that does two simple things: sends information back to IMH and receives instructions. More specifically, it sends a package of execution-related information about where the content was rendered, what device, what time, what operating system, along with an identifier that anonymously records who consumed it. It also receives a simple yes-no command to activate itself at a certain time in a certain place when a consumer's browser or device calls out to the web for instructions on the next piece of content to put in front of a user. Over time, we expect the instruction packages from IMH to become richer, moving beyond simple yes-no activation to more sophisticated guidance based on user context. For example, if motion sensors on a user's mobile device indicate that the device is moving quickly, then that likely means that the user is in transit or on a run. A smarter, context-sensitive instruction from IMH would ask the device to render the message after the user has stopped moving.

For the practitioner, there are several considerations to keep in mind as IMH-like possibilities cross your desk:

- Is the brain able to process signals from different sources and systems at varying degrees of latency—batch versus real time, for example—and use them effectively in a companion decision-making framework? This harks back to the "Can you catch what I'm pitching?" principle.

- Is the IMH's "nervous system" complete? Can the brain send signals to all the fingers, knees, and toes? Does it ensure flawless integration and interoperability across all relevant execution channels?

- How many systems can it interact with? Does it work with just social and mobile, but not set-top and desktop, for example? More important, can it seamlessly add support for future systems that are not yet known?

- How rich are the instruction sets? Do they just get and send data, or can they do more? What's the upgrade path for ensuring deeper, more intelligent experiences for consumers?

- How much latency is there? Can the IMH send instructions fast enough to deliver cooler, smarter, real-time experiences for consumers? On the other hand, can it decide when to use offline mechanisms for data transfer (like Amazon S3 and Google Cloud Storage) and when to use real-time, online HTTP APIs? (Sending ten gigabytes of data with signals from 100 million users and devices is much more efficient using S3 than making tens of millions of API requests to fulfill the data transfer in minutes for fast actionability.)

6. AN OPEN-ID ALTERNATIVE WILL TAKE ROOT, BRINGING BALANCE TO THE FORCE

We've argued that identity management is the red-hot center of modern, data-driven marketing. Right now, the Facebook-Google duopoly enjoys the deepest, widest footprint for managing consumer identity across the web, multiple devices, online and offline. Their ability to match consumers to a unique identity gives them huge power in the battle for marketers' attention and dollars.

For marketers and publishers alike, the duopoly is modestly unsettling on good days and deeply disturbing the rest of the time. What makes it particularly vexing is that the asset they control is not strictly the same as a good that's for sale, but rather a raw material that shapes the lion's share of the end good's value. Google and Facebook don't sell you per se; they sell ads, which may or may not be targeted at you. Their ability to hit their targets efficiently and on the massive channels they control gives them a nearly unfathomable advantage. And while "identity data for targeting" versus "targeted ads" might sound like a distinction without a difference, it arms them with a move-on–nothing-to-see-here narrative that, so far at least, has withstood meaningful regulatory scrutiny.

It's as if two companies owned 90 percent of the world's power generation but no one knows it, and they appear to the external market as just two very successful makers of consumer appliances that just happen to be powered by electricity. In that scenario, those two companies certainly command unbreakable market power and control the consumption and pricing of virtually all appliances and machines, not just the ones they offer themselves. The only way to counterbalance it is for other market participants to actively enable a new power provider to come into existence and to operate as a viable energy source for all players.

Possibly as a result of regulation but more likely as the natural functioning of a competitive market, we believe a neutral, trusted, nonadvertising alternative to Google-Facebook for managing consumer identity will come into existence in the next seven to ten years for the following reasons:

- The market is rapidly tilting, we believe, toward an understanding of the salience of identity data for virtually all aspects of modern business, not just marketing.

- Technology for handling and matching identity data at Facebook-Google scale is within reach. Facebook and Google are not the only ones with the technical prowess to get the job done.

- Participants with identity data that could be stitched into a fabric large enough to constitute a viable alternative are beginning to understand that (a) they can't do it themselves and (b) there are many advantages to having an independent power generator in the open market.

As modern marketers consider emerging identity solutions, they should remain attentive to the following considerations:

- **Business model conflict.** The first and most important criterion for a credible identity alternative is neutrality. In keeping with our example, are they selling just electricity, or electricity and electric appliances? Is identity management a hobby, ulterior motive, or accidental by-product of their business model? Or is it their central, espoused reason for being? A credible alternative will take steps to demonstrate that it's operating a pure "identity as a service." The winners will operate businesses unencumbered by targeted ads, commerce, content, or anything else that puts them at cross-purposes with marketer and publisher clients.

- **Depth and breadth.** When most of us refer to frozen water vapor, we call it snow. Eskimos, meanwhile, have more than 25 different words referring to the various gradations and types of snow. Identity, like snow for Eskimos, is ripe for a similar unpacking of its varieties and kinds.

Marketers looking to keep their partners honest will master this new language and cast a skeptical eye on players who make outsized claims regarding the reach and density of their identity data. A credible identity provider will speak specifically about *depth* (how much density of data the provider has within individual modalities, such as desktop, mobile, set-top, etc.) and *breadth* (how comprehensively it can connect different types of people data across those modalities). In this last case, it's particularly important to understand how a provider *bridges* identity across offline (e.g., household or phone), browser, mobile, and e-mail channels.

Remember the customer in Chapter 2 that had amassed a huge number of mobile identities but then discovered this wouldn't help it reach those same customers on browser-based channels such as desktop? This dynamic is in play for identity providers: 200 million mobile identities *sounds* impressive, but without a correspondingly high density of desktop browsers and a meaningful number of bridges between mobile and desktop browsers, it's a stranded asset. For a mobile-only marketer, an exclusive focus on mobile might constitute a value proposition that allows the marketer to differentiate its offering relative to competitors. But an identity provider that specializes in only mobile, or only e-mail, or only browser, is like a tennis player who just has a forehand but no backhand.

Breadth, the capability to see and connect users across channels and surfaces, is fundamental for any next-generation identity provider. When appraising a new identity provider, an astute marketer should seek confirmation of claims such as "We have 250 million identities under management." How many e-mail-to-mobile bridges does the provider have? How many mobile-to-desktop-browser bridges? How many online-to-offline bridges?

Provenance and Contracts

As discussed in Chapter 1, in the early days of Internet advertising, many players accumulated data in the shadows by using pixels surreptitiously placed in ads to drop cookies on users. As new channels and surfaces have emerged, the means of data collection have evolved beyond cookies and pixels, but the same general issue looms. Ill-gotten data degrades consumer trust and poses legal risk.

Accordingly, the provenance of data—where it comes from—matters as much as the quality of the data itself. Dirty data is the industry's blood diamonds. No one wants to be caught buying or selling dirty data, particularly in an evolving regulatory regime, and this is precisely why more and more marketers seek to understand the sources of their identity partner's data. Was the data accumulated via the identity provider's own infrastructure and services to its customers? Was the data purchased outright from a network of named providers? Anonymous providers? Identity providers and the marketers who work with them must understand and answer these questions of provenance.

It is responsible and necessary for marketers using identity services to understand where the data they're using actually comes from. In some cases, identity partners might have contractual limits in their own sourcing contracts that prevent them from providing particular services. Re-identification, the mapping back of a user in the open web to an e-mail identity, is a good example of something that several identity providers cannot deliver for contractual, not technical, reasons. We expect there will be other such limitations as the space takes shape.

7. CONSUMER DIRECT-DATA-SHARING FOR DOLLARS POWERED BY BLOCKCHAIN EMERGES

One of our beliefs when we started Krux was that consumers were on the cusp of rising up and taking control of their personal data signatures. We thought they would actively define what companies or other people could know about them and flock to tools that allow them to share personal information on terms of their own choosing. We envisioned a kind of inversion of today's model where individuals, not corporate behemoths, would choose to store their data in personal data vaults (PDVs) and accept payments from companies for the right to access it. One of our earliest products, called Krux Consumer, offered consumers the ability to opt out of targeting and tracking (long before opting out became a fixture of GDPR and regulatory policy) and to selectively remove particular attributes (age or zip code, for example) from the data used by external companies to target them. We made it available for free, braced ourselves for the millions of eager consumers about to flood onto our website to use it, and . . .

Crickets. We were wrong. Less than 1,000 people showed up to use Krux Consumer.

Because either we're unflagging optimists or we're just too dumb to quit, however, the idea still appeals. Its economic incentives are too immense to ignore. The ad-supported Internet has fueled companies like Google and Facebook and many others with combined market valuations of over a trillion dollars, hard evidence of the value of the data powering the ads they sell. Since the data about us is so obviously valuable, why don't we take control of it? Wouldn't that be a fairer, more productive approach?

Many bright lights have argued that we should and we will. Bill Gates suggested in 1996 that "if salespeople want to contact you and you've set a price for the privilege, they can decide whether it's worth the potential cost"[3] through analysis of whatever personal data about your preferences and propensities you've decided to make available to them and their own analysis of your unique value to them as a customer. In the *Cluetrain Manifesto*,[4] Doc Searls provocatively asserted that "we are not seats or eyeballs or end users or consumers. We are human beings, and our reach exceeds your grasp. Deal with it." Searls argues that we are not faceless consumers conscripted into the act of consumption; for him the very term "consumer" debases and disrespects us all. Rather, we are, or should be, empowered individuals with the gumption to lead, not follow, in all of our interactions with companies and vendors. Over the last decade he has advanced the concepts of vendor relationship management and the intention economy, through which everyday people could begin to assert control over their relationships with companies. In his conception, mirroring Gates's mid-1990s view, companies *earn the right* to engage with us—and they should pay us for the opportunity.

The most obvious means to that end is a data vault that gives you the ability to control your personal data signature and to share it with companies or other individuals only when you decide you want to. It would include sensitive data such as your name, birthdate, and social security number, as well as behavioral and profile data such as the content you consume, the products you buy, the influencers you follow, and so on. So much of this data is captured and monetized today not by consumers but by companies using the techniques outlined in this book. You might then naturally ask, "Why do the authors propose an idea that by its very design undermines their premise and obviates the need for so many of the technologies that butter their bread?"

Because it's cool, it's fair, and, most encouraging—it's possible.

Until now, a central obstacle has been the question of where and who. Where would personal data reside, and who would manage it? Imagine a future where you have stored your personal data in one of 200 available vaults. If you're in a checkout line waiting for a rebate to clear on your potato chip purchase in exchange for access to all your potato chip purchase information from the last six months, you need it to happen in near real time. In this scenario your data vault conducts a series of handshakes with the data clearinghouse that your store uses and fetches a particular slice of potato chip purchase data from your personal PDV, which requires meaningful computation. The more hops, the more computations, the longer you wait for the rebate to clear while you stand in the checkout line, the greater its risk of not finishing. Too many PDV managers result in a cacophony of clearinghouses and way stations, impeding the flow of data to the moments and places where it's needed. As with Visa and Mastercard, market mechanisms like this incline toward centralization.

But centralization raises hackles, here especially. A central player with the scale to compute, broker, and settle such data transactions efficiently would amass an uncomfortably huge amount of data, and thereby power, over consumers and governments. The risk of catastrophic failure cannot be ignored, particularly in an age where data breaches such as those of Experian and Target and threats from Russian and Chinese hackers loom large.

The negative consequences of a massive data spill are almost too great for us to consider—were it not for the possibilities engendered by a new technology called blockchain.

Silicon Valley is susceptible to fads and concepts hawked by true believers, so if you've heard of blockchain, it's natural for you to be skeptical. Its origins can be traced back to Bitcoin, and while enabling cryptocurrencies is one of its uses, a more general way to think of it is as a decentralized ledger that facilitates the secure tracking and settling of anything of value: fishing licenses, Furby dolls, or personal data. Importantly, as part of its essential structure, it supports something called smart contracts, which facilitate, verify, and enforce the terms of an exchange between two parties who may or may not trust each other. Blockchain's basic design, premised on the idea of radical decentralization, equips it in the most ideal way to address the control question for consumer data. By effectively flattening the clearinghouse and the PDV and distributing them across a wide fabric of computers that *collectively* perform their functions, blockchain holds the promise of enabling secure, peer-to-peer, real-time exchanges of personal data the way some of us have imagined for decades.

Back to the checkout line: To receive your rebate, you make your potato chip purchase data available on the blockchain to the store or the potato chip maker directly, without intermediaries or clearinghouses. A thin software layer takes a fraction of a penny for the service, akin to a credit card processing fee. You rest easy with the knowledge that it worked and that no one gets access to it without your express authorization, most likely in the form of a thumbprint scan on your handheld device.

The more possible things become, the more quickly they happen. Tom's initial aversion to taking pictures on his phone receded as soon as he understood how easy and convenient it was, and the same principle applies here. It is hardly a stretch to imagine that, as soon as consumers have an app on their phone that makes it easy for them to earn money from personal data, it could become as addictive as posting pics and texting friends.

The engagement possibilities that derive from consumers directly sharing data for dollars are exciting and virtually unlimited:

- Coupons, rebates, and rewards programs today account for many hundreds of billions of dollars of value exchange between brands, retailers, distributors, and consumers. By giving consumers the ability to send their personal data directly to a brand in exchange for a rebate or coupon, we remove friction and sludge from a marketspace that already exists and is ripe for a redo.

- Consider the interactive possibilities when marketers can embed a dollars-for-data widget in their ads and content. A mom in Idaho who manages the household budget and buys groceries for the family can respond to Kraft's ad with data about what her kids like to eat for dinner and earn a little extra in the process. Kraft, meanwhile, activates a durable, more personal connection with a key consumer and gathers information that can help with the near-term launch of a new food product and tailor offerings in the future for mom as her kids grow and their tastes evolve.

- Every marketer wants to know what we *actually* do, not what we say we do when we're responding to survey questions. You might cling to the idea of yourself as someone who eats fruits and vegetables because you know you should, while your purchase data might indicate a propensity to purchase more Pringles and Cheetos than you even realize. With consumer direct data sharing, consumer market research exits the peculiar realm of panels and surveys once and for all and becomes a data-driven, fact-based discipline.

- By making it easy to direct dollars from data to charities and causes, brands can engage more meaningfully with socially conscious individuals.

- Flip the setting on the app to make dollars from data available as credits for purchase of virtual goods on video games, and tens of millions of gamers jump onboard.

PUTTING IT ALL TOGETHER

We've covered a lot of ground, possibly too large an expanse to summarize in just a few pages here at the end. But you're a time-constrained practitioner, so we owe you our best shot.

The three foundational principles:

1. **Embrace the human becoming.** Let go of static concepts like unchanging segments and inflexible stages of the funnel. Your customers and audiences are leaving behind breadcrumbs that can help you engage with them in an ever-evolving, multifaceted way. Be like Meredith, which recognizes that it will never see exactly the same mom twice.

2. **You have more data than you think . . . and you think you have more data than you actually do.** Whether you believe you're sitting on a mountain of data, or you think you're hopelessly impoverished, the truth is somewhere in the middle. Build an open-eyed inventory of your data assets, the data that's hiding in plain sight as well as the missing but gatherable data within reach.

3. **There is no single truth, just more and less useful theories.** The game isn't about being right or wrong; it's about being more right than wrong as you compile a continually evolving theory of the consumer. Say

goodbye to inflexible, multiyear playbooks. Make mistakes; learn fast.

After unifying your data in and your data out in a single platform, apply the five sources of data-driven power:

1. **Segmentation.** Let a thousand flowers bloom as you define and continually redefine your customers and audiences. Use personas if they're helpful as starting points for thinking about your customer, but recognize that your competitors are going far deeper than that. Follow Heineken's lead: make your operational, day-to-day segmentation more fact-based, dynamic, and data driven.

2. **Activation.** Translate segmentation into action via activation. Say goodbye to carpet-bombing; target and measure just the audiences you want to reach across all the available channels and platforms. Know exactly where your people go. Transform the act of reaching them from a pleasant coincidence to an intentional fact.

3. **Personalization.** Build on segmentation and activation to achieve personalization in the broadest sense—cooler content, more relevant commerce, smarter selling and servicing of your customers. Follow Peugeot: paint the page in real time to give exactly *this* user what she wants.

4. **Optimization.** Adjust the velocity, pacing, reach, and frequency of your messages to achieve maximum efficiency in your marketing spend. Find the sweet spot, eliminate the long tail, nourish the short tail, and tune for recency.

5. **Insights.** Use the outputs of data-driven power sources 1–4 to accumulate richer insights about your customers. Put this data back into your marketing engine to increase precision, effectiveness, and efficiency. Fuel the self-reinforcing cycle forward.

To make it real for your organization:

- **Design and launch a data center of excellence.** Follow Turner's example: articulate a compelling strategy; identify and empower an owner; set up clear goals; and drive alignment across media, analytics, marketing performance, IT, and vendor groups.

- **Leverage the capability maturity model.** Appraise your stage realistically. Design and execute a plan to move from informal to organized to optimized.

- **Avoid the five pitfalls:**

   ○ **Absence of clear goals for data transformation.** Technology itself is not a panacea. Leverage it at the right time in concert with the right people, woven into the right process.

   ○ **Lack of a formal owner.** Empower a leader and a team to get the job done.

   ○ **Operating in a silo.** Data transformation entails coordination complexity. Break the stovepipes and preempt the tribalism that can stymie best-laid plans.

- ○ **Boiling the ocean.** Celebrate small wins to build organizational momentum. Leverage measurable results from early-stage initiatives to fund future steps.

- ○ **Failure to anticipate risk.** Remain zenlike but relentless when the inevitable glitches occur. Data pipelines will break; naysayers will grumble. Persuade constituents of the career and company benefits to them of getting behind an all-up data strategy.

When establishing a future data strategy for your organization, use the three-layer model to chart the who-what-when-where:

1. **Know.** Invest in data management to know your customers in a dynamic, 360-degree, real-time way. Reach them intelligently and with precision across every surface and every channel.

2. **Personalize.** Extend your brand and grow revenue by giving each customer more of what he wants, less of what he doesn't. Use AI and machine learning to personalize all engagement—advertising, content, commerce, sales, and service—holistically.

3. **Orchestrate.** Reach your customers at just the right time and in the right place by mapping the journey they take with your brand. Measure the effectiveness of different touchpoints in varying sequences and combinations. Intentionally craft journeys that lead to the engagement you seek.

The synchronization of know, personalize, and orchestrate is critical. Data management without AI sends the wrong signal faster. Without orchestration, we occasionally get lucky and send a relevant signal, but at the wrong time. Orchestration without AI is hard-coded scripting of a consumer journey, but without the knowledge of what journeys actually lead to the best outcomes. Winning strategies for future data transformation carefully model the interplay between know, personalize, and orchestrate.

Finally, use the seven forecasts to keep your future sensors tuned. Some will come to pass; some will miss the mark; others may catalyze new possibilities and concepts worthy of invention. Use them not as ground truth, but as starting points, to help you think about new opportunities to deliver experiences that dazzle your customer—and reinvent customer engagement. You've got this!

ACKNOWLEDGMENTS

People who work at Google call themselves Googlers. Employees of Microsoft are Microsofties. Twitter employees are Tweeps. There was a special moment when it became clear that everybody who was helping us will into existence not just a new company, but a new category, had to be more than a little nuts. For this reason (and with continued commitment to creative application of the letter K), we decided to call ourselves Krazies. When Tom sent the announcement to let everyone know that we were going to become part of Salesforce, it was directed, like every other companywide message during the prior six years, to Krazies@Krux.

Building a company from scratch is always crazy, but Krux's ambition to reinvent marketing through data and AI was uniquely audacious. This book is the distillation of intellectual capital to which we were lucky to contribute, but that so many talented Krazies created over the course of the last eight years. They are the originators of the ideas and tools shared here. We're just helpers and narrators, and we're immensely grateful to all of them.

Matt Kilmartin, Krux's revenue leader from the beginning to the end, knew how to persuade early customers to hop on board and take the journey, and he remains their most rabid advocate today. Joe Reid visited Europe to address some short-term issues and ended up staying for over three years, making us the number one data management provider on the continent. Jon Suarez Davis was the first classically trained marketer we met who understood the possibilities of the data-driven approach and was willing to bet his career on it. He continues to drive the transformation of modern marketing from his perch as chief strategy and marketing officer of Salesforce Marketing Cloud. Debra Kadner took our data integration engine apart piece by piece, put it back together again, and made it scale to support hundreds of customers.

Chris Goldsmith's big brain and appetite for complex data and consumer identity conversations helped us nourish important relationships with key customers and partners. Mike Moreau led all our early customer implementations (while we were still getting the kinks and wobbles out of our platform) and translated Tom's and Vivek's musings about peer-to-peer data flow into Krux Link, which thrives today as Salesforce Data Studio. Big ups to Xavier Zang, Paul Bates, Ted Flanagan, Jonathan Joseph, and Anupam Gupta, customer success leaders who supported the data innovators featured in our many Cases in Point and translated their experiences into frameworks for sustained success. Yacov Salomon, leader of our AI team, kept everyone honest through mathematics while overseeing the build-out of our most powerful AI and data science capabilities. Roopak Gupta oversaw the creation of every application-level feature and functionality we ever shipped. Jos Boumans led the build-out of cloud infrastructure that turned the 1,000-1 cost-performance breakthrough, theorized in the Preface, into reality. Our small, highly empowered product team, including Joydip Das, Justin Davis, Max Anderson, and Raji Bedi, relentlessly transformed specs, half-baked ideas, and market needs into working products that helped our customers achieve their grandest objectives. Max Anderson, our consumer privacy product leader, deserves a special shout-out for educating us all in the finer points of GDPR and data privacy regulations and turning them into Salesforce's winning solution for GDPR compliance and consent management.

Alex Rosen, Arthur Patterson, Nino Marakovic, Howard Charney, and Mike Galgon were not just investors, but patient mentors, thought partners, and supporters of Krux's mission at every step.

Salesforce is a special company, with a commitment to growth and innovation that enabled Krux to take root and truly flourish after our acquisition in November 2016. Marc Benioff and his cofounder Parker Harris were early, unrelenting supporters of our vision of the transformation of modern marketing through data and AI. Under their leadership, the breakthroughs we've described in this book continue to unfurl every day across hundreds of Salesforce's amazing customers. John Somorjai, head of corporate development and venture investment at Salesforce, suffered through negotiations with Tom for many months before the acquisition; and after the sale closed, John made Krux one of the fastest and most successful integrations in Salesforce history. Woodson Martin, a Salesforce veteran, grasped the opportunity for Krux and Salesforce joining together before pretty much anyone else. Chris Hecht parked his desk squarely in the middle of the tornado and got the deal done. Meghan Levin, Ryan Young, and the rest of the M&A team worked tirelessly to usher us into the Salesforce ohana. Dan Farber was an early and enthusiastic supporter of this book; without his steady guidance, it would not have come to completion.

Our editor at McGraw-Hill, Casey Ebro, helped us move with remarkable efficiency from first draft to galleys to published book. Our friend and editor, Susie Stulz, helped polish our prose and grammar; Jessica Henry upgraded our ugly sketches into helpful illustrations. We must also thank the best agent in business publishing, Jim Levine, who read our manuscript on a plane ride to Morocco a few days after our first meeting and connected us with Casey at McGraw-Hill at lightning speed.

Of course, there would be no book without our amazing customers. Our biggest thanks go to the trailblazers who trusted us to support their data-driven transformation and continue to work with us today. They are data pioneers, transforming their own careers and companies, but they are also inspiring leaders who are renovating the very nature of marketing itself. Big thanks to Ron Amram, Vice President of Media, Heineken; Douwe Bergsma, Chief Marketing Officer, Georgia-Pacific; Alysia Borsa, Chief Marketing Officer, Meredith Corporation; Ashlee Carlisle, Manager of Advanced Targeting in Media, Hershey Company; Charlie Chappell, Senior Marketing Director, Integrated Media, Hershey Company; Anita Cheung, Senior Digital and Data-Driven Marketer, RB; Mike Cunningham, Chief Information Officer, Keurig Green Mountain; Gerry D'Angelo, Director, Media Europe and Global Digital Partnerships, Mondelez; Amaya Garbayo, Director, North America Marketing Operations, Kellogg Company; Samir El Hammami, Data Driven Marketing Product Owner, Groupe PSA; Ronald den Elzen, President and CEO, Heineken USA; Aaron Fetters, SVP, Advertisers and Agencies, comScore; Jim Kizka, Associate Director, Experience Planning, Kellogg Company; Marie Gulin, Chief Marketing Officer, L'Oréal USA; Justin Herz, EVP, Digital Product, Platform and Strategy, Warner Bros. Entertainment; Nadine Karp McHugh, SVP, Omni Media, L'Oreal; Stephano Kim, EVP of Corporate Strategy, Turner; Chris Osner-Hackett, Senior Director, Global Marketing Operations, Kellogg Company; Matthew Pritchard, VP, Digital Marketing,

Campbell Soup Company; Marci Raible, VP, Global Media and Marketing Services, Campbell Soup Company; Vincent Rinaldi, Head of Addressable Media and Technology, Hershey Company; Ivelisse Roche, Associate Director, Global Media & Consumer Engagement, Mondelez; Jonny Silberman, Director of Digital Strategy and Innovation, Anheuser-Busch InBev; Gayle Smilanich, Associate Director, Media Operations, Kellogg Company; Dave Smith, SVP of Monetization and Yield, Pandora; Jon Suarez Davis, Chief Strategy Officer, Salesforce Marketing Cloud; Neil Sweeney, Founder and Chief Executive Officer, Freckle IoT; and Nuno Teles, President, Diageo Beer Company.

NOTES

Introduction

1. http://www.forbes.com/sites/greatspeculations/2016/07/19/
   k-cups-the-new-growth-driver-for-starbucks/#55470dff1d3d.
2. https://www.statista.com/statistics/326523/keurig-green
   -mountain-amount-of-brewers-sold-worldwide/.

Chapter 1

1. https://www.linkedin.com/pulse/20140709124154-47162071-the
   -evolution-of-erp-systems.
2. https://www.crmswitch.com/crm-industry/crm-industry-history/.
3. https://consumerist.com/2015/03/20/where-did-everyone-from
   -the-90s-go-when-we-all-got-facebook-and-quit-web-1-0/.
4. http://www.krux.com/customer-success/case-studies/
   ticketmaster-video/.
5. https://www.slideshare.net/KruxDigital/people-data-activation
   -from-paradox-to-paradigm-tom-chavez-data-matters-2015-las
   -vegas.
6. https://en.wikipedia.org/wiki/Mosaic_(web_browser).
7. https://www.warnerbros.com/studio/about-studio/company
   -history.
8. https://en.wikipedia.org/wiki/List_of_Warner_Bros._films.
9. http://entertainment.howstuffworks.com/movie-distribution1.htm.
10. https://techcrunch.com/2011/05/04/warner-bros-acquires-social
    -movie-site-flixster-and-rotten-tomatoes/.
11. http://www.ey.com/Publication/vwLUAssets/EY-top-10-drivers
    -impacting-global-wealth-and-asset-management/$FILE/EY-top
    -10-drivers-impacting-global-wealth-and-asset-management.pdf.
12. http://www.seattletimes.com/business/retail/coffee-pod-trend
    -has-peaked-in-us/.
13. http://money.cnn.com/2015/12/02/news/companies/target-data
    -breach-settlement.
14. https://www.nytimes.com/2015/10/07/technology/european
    -union-us-data-collection.html?_r=3.
15. https://www.wired.com/2015/10/tech-companies-can-blame
    -snowden-data-privacy-decision/.

16. http://www.wsj.com/articles/eu-u-s-agree-in-principle-on-data
-pact-1445889819.
17. https://www.wsj.com/articles/eu-u-s-agree-in-principle-on-data
-pact-1445889819.
18. https://en.wikipedia.org/wiki/General_Data_Protection
_Regulation.
19. http://adage.com/article/digital/google-gdpr-force-a-hard-choice
-publishers/313305/.
20. https://www.abine.com/blog/2012/your-facebook-friends-are
-sharing-your-info/.
21. https://blogs.wsj.com/drivers-seat/tag/shigeomi-koshimizu/.
22. https://www.globalwebindex.net/blog/digital-consumers-own
-3.64-connected-devices.
23. https://www.mobileworldlive.com/featured-content/home-banner/
connected-devices-to-hit-4-3-per-person-by-2020-report/.
24. http://www.northeastern.edu/levelblog/2016/05/13/how-much
-data-produced-every-day/.
25. http://www.bna.com/ftc-urges-internet-n57982063407/.
26. https://www.bna.com/ftc-urges-internet-n57982063407/.

Chapter 2

1. https://www.cooper.com/journal/2008/05/the_origin_of_personas.
2. https://en.wikipedia.org/wiki/AIDA_(marketing).
3. http://www.goldmansachs.com/our-thinking/pages/millennials/.
4. http://www.nielsen.com/us/en/insights/news/2016/facts-of-life
-as-they-move-through-life-stages-millennials-media-habits-are
-different.html.
5. http://www.pluck.com/wp-content/uploads/2013/08/customer
-journey-map-final-11x17inches.pdf.
6. http://www.tcs.com/resources/white_papers/PublishingImages/
TCS-Traditional-customer-lifecycle.jpg.
7. http://zenithoptimedia.ch/en/news/?id=81.
8. http://nymag.com/daily/intelligencer/2017/11/meredith-acquires
-time-inc-in-usd-2-8-billion-deal.html.
9. http://www.annualreports.com/HostedData/AnnualReports/PDF/
NYSE_K_2016.PDF.
10. http://non-gmoreport.com/articles/more-major-food-companies
-switch-to-non-gmo-ingredients/.
11. http://www.fiercepharma.com/special-report/mucinex-snot
-monster-reckitt-benckiser.
12. http://www.cbc.ca/radio/undertheinfluence/how-weather-affects
-marketing-1.2801774.

Chapter 3

1. https://www.slideshare.net/zanaida/how-brands-grow-a-summary
-of-byron-sharps-book.

2. http://www.mediapost.com/publications/article/270487/study -finds-only-40-of-digital-buys-going-to-work.html.

3. http://adage.com/article/cmo-strategy/georgia-pacific-taps -meredith-1-400-pieces-conent/300889/.

4. https://www.consumer.ftc.gov/articles/0042-online-tracking# understanding_cookies.

5. http://digitalmarketing-glossary.com/What-is-Pixel-tracking -definition.

6. http://www.forbes.com/sites/kimberlywhitler/2014/02/06/is-2014 -finally-the-year-of-mobile/#6ecb0b583e0c.

7. https://en.wikipedia.org/wiki/Moment_of_Truth_(marketing).

8. https://www.shopify.com/retail/119920451-consumers-are -showrooming-and-webrooming-your-business-heres-what-that -means-and-what-you-can-do-about-it.

9. https://apsalar.com/2015/06/all-about-idfa/.

10. https://adexchanger.com/platforms/zenith-magna-groupm -duopoly-will-capture-almost-advertising-growth-2018/.

11. https://adexchanger.com/platforms/facebook-shares-audience -data-via-carefully-controlled-clean-rooms/.

12. http://www.huffingtonpost.com/2014/03/25/coffee-chains -starbucks-dunkin_n_5006455.html.

13. https://civicscience.com/the-huge-differences-between-starbucks -and-dunkin-donuts-coffee-drinkers-part-one/.

14. https://en.wikipedia.org/wiki/Carpenter_v._United_States.

Chapter 4

1. https://adexchanger.com/data-exchanges/dmp-adoption-rise -challenges-remain.

2. http://www.cnbc.com/2014/11/07/why-those-elitist-millennials -hate-big-beer.html.

3. http://chiefmartec.com/2015/06/21-marketing-technology-stacks -shared-stackies-awards/.

4. https://www.tubemogul.com/press-releases/press-heineken-usa -names-tubemogul-exclusive-partner/.

5. http://marketrealist.com/2015/03/competitive-forces-rules-us -beer-industry/.

6. http://thefieldsofgreen.com/2014/11/20/heineken-signs-seven -mls-team-sponsorship-deals/.

7. http://www.internationalchampionscup.com/articles/pr -heineken-continues-to-build-global-soccer-presence-as -presenting-sponsor-of-international-champions-cup#tea8p TVIIywzb2FW.97.

8. http://www.sponsorship.com/IEGSR/2015/03/30/Inside -Heineken-s--Dance-More,-Drink-Slow--Campaig.aspx.

9. http://www.huffingtonpost.com/2014/07/17/neil-patrick-harris -heineken-light-_n_5596598.html.

10. https://www.iriworldwide.com/en-US/solutions/consumer-and -shopper-intelligence.
11. http://mentalfloss.com/article/56228/life-death-and-resurrection -spuds-mackenzie-original-party-animal.
12. https://www.youtube.com/watch?v=pVcbasIb8lQ.
13. https://en.wikipedia.org/wiki/Key_demographic.
14. https://medium.com/autonomous/you-likely-have-no-idea-how -tv-ratings-work-a-lot-more-people-are-watching-than-you-think -152e51657a5#.gw22wia4u.
15. http://www.pcmag.com/article2/0,2817,2402739,00.asp.
16. http://rejoiner.com/resources/amazon-recommendations-secret -selling-online/.
17. http://computer.howstuffworks.com/internet/basics/pandora.htm.
18. http://www.watermarkconsult.net/docs/Watermark-Customer -Experience-ROI-Study.pdf.
19. https://www.jitbit.com/news/bad-customer-service/.
20. https://www.fool.com/investing/general/2015/05/31/10-best-car -companies-by-auto-sales.aspx.
21. https://www.ft.com/content/08c8c462-fa7b-11e5-b3f6-11d5706 b613b.
22. http://www.krux.com/customer-success/case-studies/psa -peugeot-citroen.
23. http://www.quotationspage.com/quote/1992.html.
24. https://www.hubspot.com/marketing-statistics.
25. http://finance.yahoo.com/news/kellogg-selects-brightroll-digital -video-160000408.html.
26. http://www.nielsen.com/us/en/press-room/2015/nielsen-and -krux-collaborate-on-multi-touch-attribution-solution.html.
27. https://www.krux.com/customer-success/case-studies/kelloggs -case-study/.
28. http://www.shellypalmer.com/2015/10/non-human-traffic-ad -fraud-and-viewability/.
29. http://www.pubexec.com/post/bots-fraud-non-human-traffic -plague-top-publishers/.
30. https://www.thestreet.com/story/13161809/1/why-starbucks -should-buy-this-billion-dollar-greek-yogurt-company.html.

Chapter 7

1. http://longnow.org/seminars/02008/jan/11/embracing-uncertainty -the-secret-to-effective-forecasting/.
2. http://www.cmsmatrix.org/matrix/cms-matrix/vignette-web -content-management-now-opentext-web-experience-management.
3. *The Road Ahead,* by Bill Gates.
4. http://www.cluetrain.com/.

INDEX

A&E History Channel, power of mobile nudge, 125–126

ABI. *See* Anheuser-Busch InBev (ABI)

action in consumer sales cycle, AIDA funnel, 34–35

activation
consumer IoT and available data for, 182
data lake exports for outbound, 82
finding people across addressable channels, 79–82, 99–102
forecasting intelligent marketing hub for, 188–189
by not targeting somebody, 101–102
as source of data-driven power, 85–86, 201
striving for technical perfection before, 147
using match table, 82–83
Where (Are) My People at? and, 102–104

ad fatigue, consumer, 81

AdBright, 5

addressable channels
efficiency/effectiveness in media for, 110–115
eliminating long tail of ad f requency in, 117
finding people across, 79–82, 99–102
nourishing short tail of ad exposure in, 118–119

personalizing customer experiences, 105–107

AdForm, 5

Adidas, optimal data transformation of, 139

AdMagnet, 5

aggregation of website behavior, third-party data, 42

AI (artificial intelligence), and personalization, 158–160

AI (artificial intelligence), future forecast
next-gen CMS, 186
open-sourcing of TensorFlow, 174
overview of, 171–174
sophisticated systems of, 174–175

AIDA marketing funnel, 34–35, 155

Amazon
access to people data, 69
batch transfers of large volumes of data, 82–83
costs of capturing/processing data, 12
percentage of ad dollars going to, 149
personalization of consumers, 41, 105
revenue from recommendation engine, 105

Amram, Ron, 87–94

analytics
better segmentation across customer base, 87–88
big data, 124–125
binding execution with, 159–160

analytics (*continued*)
criteria for successful DCOE, 134
as data back in, 122–123
designing custom audiences via, 152
developing DCOE, 131–132
Hershey's magic Kiss and, 97
at informal stage of data-driven operations, 138
Internet promise of near real-time, 65
media, 124–125
power of DCOE, 129–130
Andressen, Marc, 4
Android, for consumer IoT, 184
Anheuser-Busch InBev (ABI)
digital media consortium (DMC) initiative, 112–113
granular control over message delivery, 114–115
managing reach and frequency, 111–112
media budget flow, 57
antitheft system for cars, 25
AOL, early Internet advertising of, 3
Apple iOS, for consumer IoT, 184
application programming interfaces (APIs)
consumer IoT encircles CRM, 182–183
Facebook launches Graph, 22
personalization of map, 107
artificial intelligence. *See* AI (artificial intelligence)
Audience Discovery Report, 103–104
availability
elasticity as precondition for, 176
maintaining high, 55, 66
new ways to measure data, 135
when and where aspects of, 176–178
awareness in consumer sales cycle, aida funnel, 34–35

bad actors in advertising ecosystem, finding nonhuman users, 121–122
beacons, 75–79
Bear Naked Custom Made Granola, promotion of, 124
Benckiser, Reckitt, 50–52
Bergsma, Douwe, 58–62
big data
batch data transfers on Internet of, 82–83
datafication of everything, 24–26
driving real change, 124–125
unit costs of capturing/processing data, 12
Bitcoin, origins of blockchain in, 197–200
blockchain, consumer direct data sharing, 195–200
Blue Lithium, ad network, 5
Borsa, Alysa, 38–39
bots, avoiding nonhuman users, 122
Boyle's law, inversely proportional relationships, 171
brain, of intelligent marketing hubs, 188–189
brand-awareness campaigns, and AI, 173
brands
complexity of ad technology, 56–58
costs of reacquiring churned customers, 105–106
data in. *See* data in
data out, 79–83
Dunkin' Donuts case, 71–73
eliminating long tail of ad frequency, 116–117
in era of TV ads and fewer products, 55
finding sweet spot for, 115–116
Georgia-Pacific and, 58–62
nourishing short tail of ad exposure, 118–119

breaches. *See* data breaches
breadth, of next-gen identity
    providers, 192–193
Brexit, Cambridge Analytica
    and, 21
brokers, third-party data from,
    42–43
budgets
    avoid pitfall of operating in single
        silo, 146
    bad actors extracting millions of
        online ad, 121–122
    eliminating long tail of ad
        exposure, 117
    short tail of ad impressions and,
        113, 118
    target quick wins to increase, 148
    typical flow of media, 57
business
    align data to goals of, 142–143
    data pipelining as fundamental
        to, 178
    emerging identity solutions
        conflict with, 192

Cambridge Analytica-Facebook
    debacle, 20–24, 30
Campbell Soup Company, RB and,
    50–53
"Can you catch what I'm pitching?"
    principle, 167
capability maturity model
    areas of measurement, 135–137
    data-driven performance stages,
        137
    informal stage, 138
    organized stage, 138–140
    Turner's DCOE and, 150–153
Carlisle, Ashlee, 96–97
Carpenter v. United States, 74
CDPs (customer data platforms),
        storing/refining people data
        in, 123
chaining multiple pipelines, 179

change management
    building DCOE, 129
    mitigating risk, 150
    Turner's DCOE using, 153
channels
    bridging identity across, 192–193
    measuring addressable media on,
        110–111
    orchestration in data-driven
        marketing, 160–162
Chappell, Charlie, 95–98
chief data officer (CDO), IT in
    DCOEs, 132–133
chief digital officer (CDO), hiring for
    data-driven transformation, 144
chief information officer (CIO), IT in
    DCOEs, 132–133
chief marketing officer (CMO), IT in
    DCOEs, 132–133
cloud
    Google Cloud Storage, 82–83
    next-gen CMS will be on, 186
Cluetrain Manifesto (Searls), 195–196
CMSs (content management
        systems), 185–187
combinations, handling
        orchestration via, 160
competition, new basis of
    consumer journey, 162–164
    engage (the when and where),
        160–162
    getting elephants to dance,
        166–168
    know (the who), 156–157
    overview of, 155–156
    personalize (the what), 158–160
    putting it all together, 167–168
    Subaru Australia's journey
        analysis, 164–166
    three-layer model of, 156–162
ConAgra, first- and second-party
    data of, 42
consent requirement issues,
    GDPR, 19

consideration in consumer sales cycle, AIDA funnel, 34–35

consistency, data pipelining and, 177–178

consumer direct data sharing for dollars powered by blockchain, 194–200

consumer IoT, future forecast encircles CRM, 180–184
Sonos embraces De Facto gateway for, 183–184

consumer journey
bringing it all together, 167–168
"Can you catch what I'm pitching?" principle, 166–167
overview of, 162–164
Subaru Australia's journey analysis, 164–166

consumers
behavior that transcends segmentation, 50–52
direct data sharing using blockchain, 195–200
preventing ad fatigue of, 81
real-time bidding for, 6–7
using second- and third-party data to understand, 44–46
at Warner Bros., 8–12

content management systems (CMSs), 185–187

contracts
blockchain using smart, 198
next-gen identity providers and, 194

cookies
matching advertising performance data to, 64–65
tracking specific users via, 4
using third-party data to enrich user profiles, 66–68
value of CRM records vs. anonymous, 70–71
visible to external sources, 4–5

Cooper, Alan, 34

costs, targeted marketing, 49

coupons, consumer direct data sharing and, 198

craft persona, targeted engagement, 88–89

cross-functional data sharing, as necessity, 11–12

customer data platforms (CDPs), people data in, 123

customer relationship management (CRM)
conventional vs. modern AI-enabled, 172–173
criteria for successful DCOE, 134
data captured by, 1
Dunkin' Donuts case, 71–73
encircled by consumer IoT, 180–183
orchestration, 160–162
personalization, 158–160
and purchase data, 70–71
Sonos embraces De Facto gateway, 184
"the who," 157

data
avoid single silo pitfall, 146
capability maturity model and, 136–137
cost, abundance, durability of people, 12
digital experiences beget, 12
forecast for taking control of personal, 195–197
leakage, 13–15
mitigating data transformation risk, 149
Principle 2. *See* Principle 2 (you have more data/are missing more data, than you think)
stewardship of consumer, 15–16, 30–31
unbinding content from people's, 12–13

data back in
  A&E, History Channel and,
    125–126
  insights and, 122–125
data breaches
  massive consequences of, 197
  role of IT in DCOEs, 132–133
  security promises of blockchain,
    197–200
  at Target in 2015, 15
data center of excellence (DCOE)
  at organized stage of data-driven
    excellence, 138–140
  ownership of data transformation
    via, 144
data center of excellence (DCOE),
    designing/launching
  analytics, 131–132
  criteria for success, 134
  IT, 132–133
  key stakeholders, 130
  leveraging capability maturity
    model, 135–140
  media, 129–131
  overview of, 128–129
  vendor ecosystem, 133–135
data collectors, data skimming/theft
    by, 14–15
data-driven power, five sources of
  activation, 99–104
  bringing it all together, 201–202
  insights, 122–126
  optimization. *See* optimization
  overview of, 85–87
  personalization, 104–110
  segmentation, 87–94
data in
  constructing user profiles from,
    122
  cookie data, 64–65
  CRM and purchase data, 70–71
  Dunkin' Donuts case, 71–73
  every scrap of data from every
    source, 55–58

Freckle IoT case, 75–79
  Georgia-Pacific case, 58–62
  location data, 74–75
  mobile data, 65–66
  social data, 68
  third-party data, 66–68
  understanding, 62–64
  walled gardens, 68–70
data lake exports, 82–83
data lakes, storing/refining people
    data in, 123–124
data management platforms
    (DMPs)
  assigning user ID to every person,
    79–80
  consumer IoT requiring, 180–183
  data-driven online segmentation
    using, 100–101
  data in. *See* data in
  data out, 79–83
  developing DCOE. *See* data center
    of excellence (DCOE)
  finding efficiency in addressable
    media, 111
  Fortune 500 companies
    adopting, 85
  function of, 156–157
  handling "the who" in data-
    driven marketing, 156–157
  at informal stage of data-driven
    excellence, 138
  injecting science into art of
    marketing, 61–62
  killing long tail of ad exposure,
    117
  nourishing short tail of ad
    exposure, 118–119
  unifying audience data at Turner,
    152–153
data management platforms
    (DMPs), pitfalls
  absence of clear goals, 140–143
  boiling the ocean, 147–149
  failure to anticipate risk, 149–150

data management platforms
(DMPs) (*continued*)
lack of formal owner, 143–145
operating in silo, 145–146
data out
connecting people data to every
channel, 79–82
finding people across addressable
channels, 101
finding people across channels
and systems, 122
Georgia-Pacific case, 58–62
overview of, 55–58
user matching, 82–83
data pipelining, future forecast for
2010 beliefs about sharing data, 178
availability, 176–177
chaining, 179
consistency, 177–178
consumer IoT encircles CRM
and, 182
deployment of AI systems, 174–175
elasticity, 175–176
orchestration requires effective,
179–180
pipelining defined, 175–176
self-monitoring of, 178
smart pipeline characteristics,
178–179
data-poor marketers, 124
data-rich marketers, 123
data-sharing
breach of Facebook's policies
for, 23
consumer direct, using blockchain,
195–200
first-party, 98
necessity of cross-functional, 11–12
at Pandora, 45–46
second-party, 42–43, 178
data strategy, winning
data. *See* Principle 2 (you have
more data/are missing more
data, than you think)

embrace the human becoming.
See Principle 1 (embrace the
human becoming)
overview of, 33
there is no single truth. *See*
Principle 3 (there is no
single truth, just more and
less theories)
Data Studio, 103
datafication
of everything, 24–26
managing multiple versions of
you, 26–28
managing trust/transparency,
28–32
DD Perks loyalty program, Dunkin'
Donuts, 72–73
DeFacto gateway, and consumer
IoT, 183–184
demand-side platforms
data collection events on, 14
data skimming and theft via,
14–15
orchestrating consumer journey
on, 166
vendor ecosystem and, 135
demographics
advertising new product to
certain, 35–36
developing personas based on,
157
early days of Internet advertising, 3
segmenting users based on, 34
depth, next-gen identity providers
and, 192–193
designated market areas (DMAs), 68
desire in consumer sales cycle,
AIDA funnel, 34–35
deterministic online users, 70–71
devices
A&E and power of mobile nudge,
125–126
companies need to connect to
consumers on, 39–40

consumer IoT and. *See* Consumer IoT, future forecast

customers engaging across, 36, 66

as ever-growing pool of data for capture, 26–28, 123, 133

finding people across addressable channels, 99, 101

identifying customers across, 71, 121, 152, 167–168

marketers using location data on, 74–75

measuring addressable media on, 110–112

mobile phones as miraculous marketing, 65–66

next-gen CMS capability across, 186

Pandora learns about listeners via, 44–46

digital media consortium (DMC) initiative, 112–113

digital signatures, people data via, 2

digitization, datafication vs., 24–25

display advertising

data in/data out. *See* data in; data out

finding people across addressable channels, 99–102

Georgia-Pacific moves from scarcity to abundance, 58–62

LUMAscape map shows complexity of, 56–57

typical flow of media budgets for, 57–58

DMAs (designated market areas), 68

DMC (digital media consortium) initiative, 112–113

Dunkin' Donuts

brand awareness through touch-points, 81–82

data in, 71–73

dynamic content, next-gen CMSs, 187

effectiveness, in addressable media, 110–115

efficiency, in addressable media, 110–115

elasticity, and data pipelining, 176

elections, Cambridge Analytica and U.K./U.S., 21

engage (the when and where), three-layer competition model, 160–162

enterprise resource systems, 1

European (EU) privacy regulations

EU Safe Harbor, 16–17

Global Data Protection Regulation (GDPR), 18–20, 133–134

role of IT in DCOEs, 133

vs. United States, 15–16

eventual consistency, data pipelining and, 177–178

Facebook

access to people data, 69

ad-supported Internet fueling, 195

Cambridge Analytica debacle, 20–24, 30

data out to, 80, 101

managing identity data, 190–191

marketers leveraging social data on, 68

percentage of ad dollars going to, 149

targeted marketing of, 49

turning preferences/profiles into data, 24

as walled garden, 68–70

Family Rewards program, Kellogg's, 40–41

first-party data

aligning with driving customer experience, 107

beliefs in 2010 about, 178

Dunkin' Donuts and, 72–73

greater relative value in, 43

Hershey's magic Kiss and, 96–98

first-party data (*continued*)
mapping in Audience Discovery
Report, 103
Turner's DCOE and, 151–152
as underestimated source of
power, 41–42
Flixster, Warner Bros. and, 11
forecasts. *See* future, seven forecasts
for
foundational principles
for building winning data strategy,
33
embrace the human becoming.
See Principle 1 (embrace the
human becoming)
summary of, 200–201
there is no single truth. *See*
Principle 3 (there is no single
truth, just more and less
theories)
you have more data/and are
missing data. *See* Principle
2 (you have more data/are
missing more data, than you
think)
Freckle IoT case, 75–79
frequency analysis, ad delivery
analyzing range of frequency,
112–114
recency analysis as part of,
119–120
viewability layer finding
nonhuman users, 122
frequency management, ad
delivery
analyzing range of frequency,
112–114
finding efficiency in addressable
media, 111
finding sweet spot for brands,
115–116
maintaining people-based view,
120–121
overview of, 111–112

frequent pattern analysis, data
mining, 110
future, seven forecasts for
all-in-one intelligent marketing
hub, 187–190
artificial intelligence, 171–174
consumer direct-data-sharing
powered by blockchain,
194–200
consumer IoT encircles CRM,
180–184
content management, 185–187
data pipelining, 174–180
open-ID alternative, 190–194
overview of, 169–170

Gates, Bill, 195
GDM. *See* global delivery management (GDM)
GDPR. *See* Global Data Protection
Regulation (GDPR), EU
Geofencing, and Freckle IoT, 77
Georgia-Pacific
eliminating long tail of ad
frequency, 117
moving from scarcity to abundance,
58–62
Global Data Protection Regulation
(GDPR), EU
consent requirement issues, 19
"right to be forgotten," 18–19
"right to explanation," 20
role of IT in DCOEs, 133–134
global delivery management (GDM)
bad actors in advertising
ecosystem and, 121–122
controlling frequency of messages,
81
coordinating frequency and
recency, 120–121
instructing channels to suppress
users, 117
transferring data out in near real
time, 83

goals
    AI and time to specify campaign,
       173
    capability maturity model metrics
       for success, 136–137
    pitfall of operating in single silo,
       146
    pitfalls of data transformation,
       140–143
    stack-ranking, 148–149
Google
    access to people data, 69
    ad-supported Internet fueling, 195
    Android as gateway for consumer
       IoT, 184
    Cloud Storage, 82–83
    managing identity data, 190–191
    open-sourcing TensorFlow,
       174–175
    percentage of ad dollars going
       to, 149
    turning affinities/curiosities into
       data, 24
    unit costs of capturing/processing
       data, 12
    as walled garden, 68–70
GPS (global positioning system), turns
    location into data, 24, 74–75
Graph API tool, Facebook, 22–23
Gulin, Marie, 139

Hammami, Samir El, 108–110
Harris, Neil Patrick, 92
hashing, in onboarding, 70
Heineken
    challenges for, 91–93
    delivering customized content, 1
    segmentation study, 87–89
    synthesizing data/building
       customers, 93–94
    using TicketMaster/Live Nation
       data, 178–179
    vision for addressable market,
       90–91

Heraclitus, 33–34
Hershey, Milton, 95
Hershey's magic Kiss, 95–98
Herz, Justin, 10
History Channel, power of mobile
    nudge, 125–126
How Brands Grow (Sharp), 55
Hubspot, marketing automation
    provider, 111

identity
    bridging across channels, 192–193
    consumer IoT encircles CRM,
       182–183
    forecast for open-ID alternative,
       190–194
    managing multiple versions of
       you, 26–28
    mapping inbound and outbound,
       80
informal stage, data-driven
    operations, 138
insights
    A&E History Channel and, 125–126
    analyst role in DCOEs, 131–132
    as data back in again, 122–125
    as source of data-driven power,
       86, 202
Instagram, leveraging social data
    on, 68
instruction sets, intelligent marketing
    hubs, 189
intelligent marketing hub (IMH),
    future forecast for, 187–190
interest in consumer sales cycle,
    AIDA funnel, 34–35
intermediaries, data skimming/
    theft via, 14–15
Internet advertising
    emergence of ad networks, 5–6
    eroding cost efficiency of, 7–8
    European privacy regulations,
       16–20
    evolution at Warner Bros., 8–12

Internet advertising (*continued*)
  in mid- to late 1990s, 3–4
  people data generated by, 2
  real-time bidding for customers, 6–7
  threats to privacy/security, 12–16
  tracking users via cookies, 4–5
  very early days of, 3
  at Warner Bros., 8–12
Internet Explorer, digital advertising, 4
Internet of Things (IoT)
  CRM encircled by consumer, 180–183
  massive data flow of, 29
inversely proportional relationship, AI and workflow, 171–174
IT (information technology)
  complexity of ad technology, 56–58
  developing DCOE, 132–134
  organizational adoption and, 129

jargon, complexity of ad, 56–57
JetBlue, 123
Juice Mobile, 75–76

Kawaja, Terence, 56–58
Kellog Company
  ad frequency management, 111–112, 114–115
  Bear Naked Custom Made Granola and, 124
  eliminating long tail of ad frequency, 117
  had more data than they thought, 40–42
  missing target creates opportunities, 48
  suppressing users/nonhuman traffic, 148
  targeted marketing at scale, 47–48
key performance indicators (KPIs)
  building framework, 142

data transformation with goals for, 141
finding sweet spot for brands, 115–116
in optimized stage of data-driven excellence, 140
role of media team in DCOES, 130
Kim, Stephano, 151–153
know (the who), three-layer competition model, 156–157
Kogan, Aleksandr, 22–23
Koshimizu, Shigeomi, 25
Krux Consumer, 195

latency
  of intelligent marketing hubs, 189–190
  orchestration and mismatches of, 179–180
laws, role of IT in DCOEs, 132–133
leadership, in data-driven marketing, 127
leakage, data, 13–15
Lewis, E. St. Elmo, 34–35
location data
  Freckle IoT helps fans before game, 75–79
  tracking users via, 74–75
long tail of ad impressions
  eliminating, 116–117
  overexposed users receiving, 114
L'Oréal USA
  optimal data transformation of, 139
  Where (Are) My People at? and, 102–104
loyalists persona, targeted engagement, 89
LUMAscape map (Kawaja), ad technology, 56–58

mainstream persona, targeted engagement, 88
Makeup Genius app, L'Oréal USA, 139

marketers
  continual need to expand data, 43
  costs of Internet advertising, 7–8
  creating integrated media for
    consumers, 43
  effect of programmatic media
    on, 7
  improving data governance for
    consumers, 15
  prioritizing trust and transparency,
    31–32
media
  advertising product to demo-
    graphic, 35–36
  buying audiences separately
    from, 5–6
  criteria for successful DCOE, 134
  developing DCOE, 129–131
  efficiency/effectiveness in
    addressable, 110–115
  optimization across channels,
    173–174
Meredith
  Georgia-Pacific partners with,
    60–61
  optimal data transformation of,
    139
  redefines "Momness" case, 38–39
Microsoft
  blue screen of death, 178
  digital advertising in late 1990s,
    3–4
  unit costs of capturing/processing
    data, 12
mobile nudge effect, 65–66, 126
Model Clauses, EU Safe Harbor,
    17–18
Mondelez, Freckle IoT and, 76–79
monitoring, data pipelines as self,
    178
Mosaic, limitless digital advertising
    of, 3–4
MSN, early Internet advertising of, 3
Mucinex, 50–53

Music Genome Project, Pandora,
    45, 105

nervous system, of intelligent
    marketing hubs, 188–189
Netflix, mastery of personalization,
    41, 104–105
Netscape, digital advertising of, 3–4
Nielsen, digital media consortium
    initiative, 112–113

observational bias, segmentation
    and, 49
onboarding, definition, 71
open-ID alternative, future forecast
    for, 190–194
optimization
  efficiency/effectiveness in
    addressable media, 110–115
  eliminating long tail, 116–117
  finding sweet spot, 115–116
  nourishing short tail, 118–119
  people-based view of frequency,
    120–122
  as source of data-driven power,
    86, 201
  tuning for recency, 119–120
optimized stage, data-driven
    operation, 139–140
orchestration
  in data-driven marketing, 160–162
  effective pipelining and, 179–180
organization, make it real for your
  bringing it all together, 202–203
  capability maturity model, 135–140
  DCOE at Turner example, 150–153
  designing/launching DCOE,
    128–135
  overview of, 127–128
  pitfalls, absence of clear goals,
    140–143
  pitfalls, boiling the ocean, 147–149
  pitfalls, failure to anticipate risk,
    149–150

organization, make it real for your (*continued*)
pitfalls, lack of formal owner, 143–145
pitfalls, operating in silo, 145–146
organizational alignment, and privacy policies, 29–30
organized stage, data-driven operation, 138–139
ownership (general contractor)
as data transformation requirement, 143–145
smarter pipelines enforcing, 179

Pandora
optimal data transformation of, 139–140
personalizing consumer tastes, 105
using second- and third-party data, 44–46
people data
capability maturity model metrics for, 136–137
as competitive advantage, 124–125
connecting to every channel, 79–82
customized content delivery, 1–2
datafication of everything and, 24–26
from digital signatures, 2
European privacy regulations, 16–20
Facebook-Cambridge Analytica and, 20–24
history of, 1
identity/multiple versions of you, 26–28
Internet advertising and. *See* Internet advertising
organizational adoption and, 129
threats to consumer privacy/security, 12–16
trust and transparency in datafied world, 28–32

walled gardens and, 69
as "the who" in data-driven marketing, 156–157
personal data vaults (PDVs), consumer direct-data-sharing, 195–200
personalization
next-gen CMSs and, 186–187
Peugeot lures consumers to showroom, 107–110
as source of data-driven power, 86, 201
tension between privacy and, 15–16, 20
using data to build customer experience, 104–107
personalize (the what), in three-layer competition model, 158–160
personas
concept does not work in today's world, 37–38
developing in segmentation, 34
Heineken's targeted engagement strategy, 88–89
petabytes of data, consumer IoT encircles CRM, 182
Peugeot, lures consumers to showroom, 107–110
physical availability, branding and, 55
Principle 1 (embrace the human becoming)
anticipating changes in consumer tastes, 47
bringing it all together, 200
in Heineken's segmentation study, 89, 94
Meredith redefines "Momness," 38–39
rejecting rigid labels for consumers, 37–38, 40
unlearning segmentation/funnel concepts, 34–37

Principle 2 (you have more data/are missing more data, than you think)
  bringing it all together, 200
  Dunkin' Donuts confronts, 72
  Georgia-Pacific confronts, 62
  Hershey internalizes power of, 98
  overview of, 40–44
Principle 3 (there is no single truth, just more and less theories)
  bringing it all together, 200–201
  finding sweet spot for brands, 115–116
  Heineken puts into practice, 91–92
  overview of, 46–50
  RB and Campbell Soup Company, 50–53
  translates human becoming into action, 47
privacy
  European regulations for, 16–20
  Facebook-Cambridge Analytica debacle, 20–24
  hiring top-notch counsel for, 29
  improving data governance for consumers, 15
  personalization and, 15–16
  role of IT in DCOEs, 132–133
  smarter pipelines/compliance with, 179
  threats to consumer, 12–16
  walled gardens and, 68–70
privacy policies
  in organizational alignment, 29–30
  posting privacy promise along with, 31
  trust/transparency in datafied world and, 29
probabilistic online users, deterministic signals vs., 70–71
processes
  capability maturity model metrics for, 136–137
  organizational adoption and, 129

profitability, impact of customer experience on, 106
programmatic media, Internet advertising, 6–7
prospective look-alikes, 81–83
provenance of data, next-gen identity providers, 193–194
purchase data
  big data analytics of, 124
  consumer direct data sharing and, 199
  CRM and, 70–71, 73
  data providers selling, 67
  Dunkin' Donuts and, 71–73
  as first-party data, 123
  Hershey Company and, 97
  highly modeled today, 79
  mobile payments connect marketers with, 66

quick wins, to avoid transforming too quickly, 148

radical decentralization, blockchain based on, 198
RB and the Campbell Soup Company, 50–53
real-time bidding for customers, 6–7
reason to believe (RTB), in data-driven marketing, 127
rebates, consumer direct data sharing and, 198
recency, tuning ad delivery to, 119–120
revenue, customer experience and, 106
"right to be forgotten," GDPR, 18–19
"right to explanation," GDPR, 20
Rinaldi, Vincent, 97–98
Risk mitigation, data transformation, 149–150
Road map, avoid transforming too quickly via, 148
Rule-based execution, next-gen CMSs, 186

SaaS (Software as a service), 185, 186
Safe Harbor, EU, 16–17
Sales cycle, how consumers move
    through, 34–35
Salesforce
    building marketing cloud for
        one-stop shop, 168
    criteria for successful DCOE, 134
    Data Studio visualization tool, 103
    finding sweet spot for brand, 116
    frequency analysis of typical
        campaign, 113
    frequency and recency, 120
    journey insights report for travel
        site, 164, 166
    law of workflow, 171
    pay as you go model for SaaS, 185
    power of DCOE, 130
    segmentation menu in DMP, 67
    sources of value in data-driven
        marketing, 86
    stages of data-driven operation,
        147
    three-layer model of competition,
        156
    trust practices of, 31
Salomon, Yacov, 119–120
scammers, advertising, 121–122
schema-on-read semantics, 182
schema-on-write systems, 182
science, in art of marketing, 61–62
scut time, modern AI reduces, 1
    72–173
Searls, Doc, 196
second-party data
    mapping in Audience Discovery
        Report, 103
    from named partner with
        data-sharing agreement,
        42–43
    Pandora using third-party and,
        44–46
    sharing relationships with chosen
        partners, 178

Turner's DCOE and, 152
security, threats to consumer, 20–24
segmentation
    addressing challenges, 91–93
    concept does not work in today's
        world, 37–38
    consumer behavior that transcends,
        50–53
    deploying deeper analytics for
        better, 87–88
    Dunkin' Donuts and, 71–73
    envisioning total addressable
        market, 90–91
    Hershey's magic Kiss and, 95–98
    Meredith redefines "Momness"
        and, 38–39
    observational bias and, 49
    revenue strategy of data-driven
        online, 100–101
    smarter pipelines enforce
        predefined, 179
    as source of data-driven power,
        85, 201
    synthesizing data/building
        customers, 93–94
    targeting distinct personas, 88–89
    unlearning concept of, 34
    using third-party data, 42–43,
        66–68
self-healing, elasticity as
    precondition for, 176
self-monitoring, of data pipelines,
    178
sequences, for orchestration in data-
    driven marketing, 160–162
Sharp, Byron, 55
short tail of ad impressions
    nourishing, 118–119
    underexposed users receiving, 113
signals of intent, CRM records as,
    70–71
Silberman, Jonny, 111–112, 127
silos, avoid pitfall of operating in
    single, 145–146

skimming data, 14

smart contracts, blockchain, 198

smartphones
  accessing phone numbers in
      CRM, 70
  data from, 65–66
  Freckle IoT helps fans find
      Velveeta before game, 75–79
  location data from, 74–75
  "Take Back the Table" campaign
      and, 60–61

Smith, David, 45–46

Snot Monster mascot, RB and the
    Campbell Soup Company,
    50–51

Snowden, Edward, privacy issues
    exposed by, 16

social data
  channel control by a few
      oligopolists, 161
  leveraged by marketers, 68

Software as a service (SaaS), 185,
    186

Sonos, consumer IoT and, 183–184

stakeholders
  DCOE, 130
  using correct, 141

Starbucks, 71–73

strategy, modern AI enables time
    for, 172–173

Suárez-Davis, Jon, 47–48, 111

subscription service, next-gen CMS
    marketed as, 186

success
  capability maturity model for
      DCOEs, 135–140
  criteria for DCOEs, 134

survey-based metrics, 104

Sweeney, Neil, 75–79

sweet spot of ad impressions, 114–116

"Take Back the Table" campaign,
    60–61

Target, data breach in 2015, 15

targeted marketing
  controlling delivery of
      cross-channel messages, 114
  as expensive, 49
  Facebook, 49
  implementing at scale, 47–48
  RB and the Campbell Soup
      Company, 50–53
  segmentation leads to observa-
      tional bias, 49

technology. *See* IT (information
    technology)

TensorFlow, Google open sources,
    174–175

theft, data, 14

third-party data
  beliefs in 2010 about, 178
  data in, 66–68
  Hershey's magic Kiss and, 97
  mapping in Audience Discovery
      Report, 103
  Pandora using both second-party
      and, 44–46
  purchasing from data brokers,
      42–43
  Turner's DCOE and, 152

threats, to consumer privacy/
    security, 12–16

three-layer model, future data
    strategy
  bringing it all together, 167–168,
      203–204
  engage, 160–162
  know, 156–157
  as new basis of competition, 156
  personalize, 158–160

TicketMaster/Live Nation
  delivering customized content to
      people, 1
  second-party data sharing,
      178–179

TIE fighter drawing
  connecting people data to every
      channel, 80

TIE fighter drawing (*continued*)
  data management platforms
    (DMPs), 63–64
  user matching and, 82
tools, capability maturity model
    metrics, 136–137
transparency
  in datafied world, 28–32
  role of IT in DCOEs, 132–133
Trump, Donald, 21
trust
  in datafied world, 28–32
  improving data governance, 15
  role of IT in DCOEs, 132–133
truth. *See* Principle 3 (there is no
    single truth, just more and less
    theories)
Turner
  Data Cloud, 152–153
  DCOE, 150–153
  optimal data transformation
    of, 139
Twitter Fail Whale, 178

United States v. Carpenter, 74
user IDs
  data management systems assign
    to every user, 79
  DMPs connecting across multiple
    platforms, 117
  forecasting open-ID alternative
    for, 190–194
  linking for ad frequency manage-
    ment, 111, 121
  user matching via, 82

vendors
  "Can you catch what I'm
    pitching?" principle,
    166–167
  developing DCOE, 133–135
  third-party data. *See* third-party
    data
viewability campaign layer, to find
    nonhuman users, 122
vignette, developing CMS, 185
Vikings, mobile nudge effect,
    125–126

walled gardens, data protection in,
    68–70
WAMPA (Where (Are) My People
    At?), 102–104
Wanamaker, John, 110, 113
Warner Bros., 8–12, 81
Watermark Groups, and personal-
    ization, 105
weather forecast data, Campbell's
    soup case, 51–52
website behavior, aggregation
    of, 42
workflow, inversely proportional
    relationship of AI and,
    171–174
Wylie, Chris, 21

Yahoo! early days of Internet
    advertising, 3

Zuckerberg, Mark, 21

ABOUT THE AUTHORS

TOM CHAVEZ

Tom Chavez is the founder and CEO of Superset Inc., a venture studio that founds, funds, and builds technology companies. He was the cofounder and CEO of Krux, acquired by Salesforce in 2016. Previously, Tom worked at Microsoft as a general manager in Microsoft's Advertiser and Publisher Solutions group after the acquisition of Rapt, where he served as founder and CEO from 1999 to 2007. Tom also worked at Rockwell Palo Alto Laboratory as a researcher in probabilistic AI and decision theory and later in the operations and networking groups at Sun Microsystems. He holds an engineering PhD from Stanford University and an AB in computer science and philosophy from Harvard University.

CHRIS O'HARA

Chris O'Hara is one of the world's most widely published writers on digital marketing and data transformation for marketing. His "Managing the Data" *AdExchanger* column and annual feature-length Econsultancy white papers on programmatic media, data management, mobile advertising, and media management are widely read throughout the ad technology, media, and agency worlds. Chris joined Krux to build and lead its marketer data practice. Chris now oversees global product marketing for Salesforce DMP, Data Studio, Ad Studio, Social Studio, and emerging data products for the Salesforce Marketing Cloud. Chris is the author of six bestselling books on food and drink, including *The Bloody Mary* and *Great American Beer*, an exploration of America's domestic beer brands and how they were marketed into mainstream consciousness. Chris and his books have been featured on NBC's *The Today Show*, on *The CBS Morning Show,* and in the *Wall Street Journal* and *Esquire*.

VIVEK VAIDYA

Vivek Vaidya is a serial tech entrepreneur who has spent the last 25 years building industry-leading technologies in enterprise software, data management, analytics, and machine learning/ AI. In his most recent role as CTO of Salesforce Marketing Cloud, he led and managed the engineering teams for all Salesforce Marketing Cloud products. Vivek joined Salesforce in 2016 through the acquisition of Krux, of which he was cofounder and CTO. Previously, he also served as CTO of Rapt, Inc., which was acquired by Microsoft in 2008. Vivek has extensive expertise in algorithms, data mining, machine learning technologies, networking and distributed systems, and enterprise software systems. He holds an MS in Computer Science from the University of Denver and an MS in Mathematics and Computer Applications from the Indian Institute of Technology, Delhi.